Handmade DELIGHTS BRIGHTEN UP HOMES...INSIDE AND OUT

Liven up your garden, create a heartwarming balcony and welcome guests to your front porch with outdoor decor and accessories you personally created. With the all-new **Handmade Outdoor Crafts** you'll discover how easy (and fun) it is to take your love of crafting outside.

From cute ladybug accents to mosaic flowerpots, the simply adorable projects found here make it a snap to give a one-of-a-kind touch to your yard. You'll even find crafts that bring your love of the outdoors inside! Decorate your home with nature-inspired art, festive wreaths, smart centerpieces and more.

Take a look inside and you'll find:

- **71 crafts** to personalize gardens, decks, patios and other spaces

- Dozens of **upcycled projects** that give new life to secondhand treasures

- **Hints and tips** to take your crafting to the next level, beat the clock and save money

- Step-by-step **directions** and **materials lists** of readily available items

Whether you're looking to spruce up a shade garden, illuminate a pathway or decorate a windowsill, the ideas in **Handmade Outdoor Crafts** turn dream yards into realities while turning houses into homes.

TASTE OF HOME BOOKS • RDA ENTHUSIAST BRANDS, LLC • MILWAUKEE, WI

93

© 2020 RDA Enthusiast Brands, LLC.
1610 N. 2nd St., Suite 102
Milwaukee WI 53212-3906

Visit us at **tasteofhome.com** for other
Taste of Home books and products.

ISBNs:
978-1-61765-895-2 (Trade)
978-1-61765-943-0 (DTC)

LOCC: 2019950032

Component Number: PR00008073

Executive Editor: Mark Hagen
Senior Art Director: Raeann Thompson
Editor: Christine Rukavena
Designers: Jazmin Delgado, Arielle Jardine
Copy Chief: Deb Warlaumont Mulvey

Pictured on front cover:
Retread & Grow, p. 46

Cover Photography: Taste of Home Photo Studio

**Pictured on back cover
(clockwise from top left):**
Stars at Night, p. 26; Moss Letter Art, p. 92;
Bowling Ball Bugs, p. 20; Stick 'em Up, p. 74;
Bowling Pin Butterfly, p. 8; Country Place Mats,
p. 94; Tin Can Herb Set, p. 95; Pup Primping
Station, p. 77

Printed in China.
1 3 5 7 9 10 8 6 4 2

70

35

61

CONTENTS

More ways to connect with us:

BACKYARD *Magic*

HANDMADE HELPER
Want even taller mushrooms?
Plant more pots in various sizes
and stack them. Place a drain
plate on the top of each stack.

GARDEN MUSHROOMS

Dress up your yard, garden or porch with these quick and easy painted mushrooms. They're lightweight and can be moved to add color to different parts of your yard. Use any old pots you have on hand or, for a faster project, buy prepainted pots and add the painted dots. This project is so simple that it's great for kids, too!

MATERIALS

- **Spray paint, in white, and in choice of colors for mushroom tops**
- **2-3 round terra-cotta pots in various sizes**
- **2-3 round terra-cotta drain plates (each 3-5 in. wider than the bottom of matching pot)**
- **2-in.-wide round sponge or spouncer**
- **White acrylic craft paint**
- **Small paintbrush**
- **Waterproof clear paint or spray sealer**
- **Epoxy or waterproof outdoor glue, optional**

DIRECTIONS

1. In a well-ventilated area, spray-paint the exterior of the pots white and the underside of each drain plate in a contrasting color. Apply as many coats as needed for full coverage; let pots and plates dry 24-48 hours.
2. For the dots on the mushroom tops, dip a round sponge or spouncer in white acrylic paint. Coat it liberally and then press it to a painted drain plate. Remove quickly, leaving a white dot. If needed, use a small paintbrush to fill in any light areas of paint.
3. Repeat Step 2, making several randomly placed white dots on each painted drain plate. Let all the dots dry completely.
4. Coat all the painted surfaces with a layer of clear waterproof sealer. Let dry 24-48 hours.
5. To assemble the mushrooms, center a drain plate, painted side up, on top of each upside-down pot. For stability, use epoxy or waterproof outdoor glue to adhere the drain plate to the base.

MINIATURE POND

Create a calming oasis with an easy, do-it-yourself pond. You don't even need fancy pumps—just a handful of materials, water and the right plants.

MATERIALS

- **Watertight container**
- **Garden soil or aquatic plant soil**
- **Water plants (see list below)**
- **Black plastic pots**
- **Pea gravel (if using garden soil)**
- **Fertilizer tabs (if using aquatic plant soil)**
- **Small bricks or small ceramic pots**
- **Mosquito Dunks doughnut**

THE PLANTS

You'll need 3 types of aquatic plants:
- **Emergents** have great foliage. Try umbrella palm and dwarf cattails.
- **Submerged** live below the surface of the water and add oxygen. Try anacharis.
- **Floaters** rest on the water's surface. Water hyacinth and parrot's feathers are good options.

DIRECTIONS

1. Choose your watertight container. Materials like ceramic, concrete, plastic, terra cotta, metal or porcelain are great options. Don't use wood unless you line it with black plastic. Remember that the pot will get heavy, so place it where you want to display it before filling it with water.
2. Use soil to set the emergents and submerged plants in black plastic pots. If you use garden soil, cover it with 1-2 in. of pea gravel to keep it from floating to the top. If using aquatic plant soil, bury a fertilizer tab with each plant.
3. Place potted plants at the appropriate depths in the empty pond container on bricks or upside-down ceramic pots. Plant from deep to shallow, and from large to small.
4. Add water to the potted plants, then fill the container itself.
5. Once the container is full of water, add floater plants and a Mosquito Dunks doughnut.

BOWLING PIN BUTTERFLY

An old bowling pin can metamorphose into a beautiful butterfly with this striking pair of wings made from plywood. Use the free downloadable stencil (see link in Step 1), and let your imagination soar when you paint your own wing patterns.

MATERIALS

- Printer, optional
- Pre-primed lauan plywood
- Four L-brackets and screws
- Medium- or fine-grit sandpaper
- Bowling pin
- Stiff wire or coat hanger for antennae
- Galvanized wire for hanging
- Primer
- Spray paint
- Acrylic craft paints
- Exterior-grade spray varnish
- Paintbrush
- Super glue
- Needle-nose pliers
- Craft knife
- Drill and small bit
- Jigsaw

DIRECTIONS

1. Enlarge to desired size and tile-print the free downloadable wing stencil at *birdsandblooms.com/bowlingbutterfly*. Or draw the butterfly wing freehand.

2. Carefully cut out the wing stencil and, if desired, the inner detailing. Trace outline and detailing onto the plywood with a pencil, then flip the stencil and repeat to create wings that are mirror images of each other.

3. Using a jigsaw, cut out the wings. Lightly sand the wings until smooth.

4. Prep bowling pin by drilling 2 holes for antennae in the top using a drill bit slightly larger than the diameter of wire.

5. Prime the bowling pin or use a spray paint with primer. Spray paint the bowling pin and let dry completely.

6. Paint wing design using acrylic paint and let dry completely.

7. Drill holes on side of bowling pin to affix wings. Attach wings using screws and 2 L-brackets per wing. (See Photo 1.)

8. Center a screw to the back of the bowling pin for hanging. Using needle-nose pliers, wrap galvanized wire around the head of the screw to form a loop. (See Photo 2.)

9. Cut wire antennae to desired length, then use pliers to twist ends, forming a small decorative loop on each. Drop small amounts of glue into antenna holes, then insert antennae. Keep butterfly upright until glue dries.

10. Spray butterfly with several coats of exterior-grade spray varnish. Once dry, hang and properly secure butterfly to a gardening shed, fence or tree.

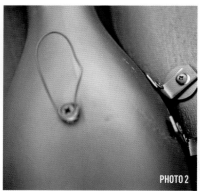

PHOTO 1

PHOTO 2

BUTTON-EYED SUSAN

This funky flower is crafted from a soda pop can, buttons and rebar, but whatever you have around the house can work. Use additional soda cans to add extra petals to the back of the flower if you'd like.

MATERIALS

- Soda pop can
- Buttons
- Spray paint
- Weatherproof glue
- Rebar
- Safety gloves

DIRECTIONS

1. Wearing safety gloves, cut petal-shaped strips down the sides of soda can, stopping at bottom of can. Carefully bend and flatten strips to lay evenly with rounded bottom of can.
2. Spray-paint the flattened can and let dry completely.
3. Using weatherproof glue, attach buttons to center of flower and rebar to back of flower.

WHIMSICAL FAIRY GARDEN

Invite a little magic into your backyard with a fairy garden. Begin by deciding whether your fairies deserve a formal environment or something more casual. Maybe you have something exotic in mind, like a Gothic manor or a tropical paradise on the beach. Whether you set your magical world in a container or out in your garden, it will surely charm visitors of all ages.

MATERIALS
- Planting container
- Container soil mix
- Plants (see list below)
- Miniature garden accessories

PLANTS
- Stonecrop sedum
- Elfin thyme
- White moss thyme
- Corsican mint
- Hen-and-chicks
- Irish moss
- Angel's tears
- Ornamental strawberry
- Creeping veronica
- Green mound juniper
- Satsuki azalea
- Ginkgo

DIRECTIONS

1. Choose the location first, as this will determine the plants needed to fill in the fairy garden.

2. Pick a container. Just about anything you can plant in is suitable, but keep in mind you want enough depth to maintain soil moisture, particularly in a sunny spot; enough surface area to accommodate all the elements you envision; and a few drainage holes.

3. Sketch out the garden on paper, and then choose plants that look mature in miniature. Plants that offer variations in height and texture give fairy gardens a natural, cohesive look.

4. Using photo as a guideline, set plants into container garden with soil mix.

5. Add or carve out features such as pebble walkways, mini flagstone patios, sandy beaches or dry creek beds.

6. Add a few miniature garden accessories as desired.

> ### HANDMADE HELPER
> Avoid the temptation to overdo it when it comes to cute fairy garden accessories. Instead, select a few key trinkets and place them naturally among your plants for a truly whimsical spot that will get smiles from guests of all sizes!

CRAFT: DAISY SISKIN, LITTLEHOUSEINTHESUBURBS.COM

• • •

BEADED WIND CHIME

Relax with the soothing sounds of this wind chime you crafted from an old teapot, silverware and beads. It helps to have a little experience in beading to make the strands, but even if you don't, this is a great project to get you started. This design calls for a vintage teapot, but you can also use an old sugar bowl, gravy boat or any other classic dining accessory you might have on hand. Let your imagination lead the way for this delightful craft.

MATERIALS
- **Vintage teapot**
- **Silver-plated flatware, 5 pieces**
- **Formula 409 cleaner**
- **Black permanent marker**
- **Bench drill**
- **³⁄₃₂-in. drill bit**
- **Tiger tail jewelry wire, about 60 in.**
- **Glass beads, assorted**
- **Crimps and end pieces for jewelry beading**
- **Fishing tackle parts (a crimp and a snap swivel)**
- **Pliers**

DIRECTIONS

1. Using cleaner, remove any dirt, dust or grime from the teapot and flatware.
2. Decide where the chimes will hang best from the bottom of the teapot. (For this teapot, 4 chimes were set around the outside perimeter and 1 chime was hung from the center.) Mark all of the hole locations with a black permanent marker.
3. Similarly, mark the spots on the top of the teapot where the beaded strands for hanging will be placed. (For most teapots, 4 evenly spaced points will probably be best.)
4. Drill each marked hole with the bench drill and drill bit. Drill a hole at the bottom (stem end) of each piece of silverware.
5. Cut the wire to desired lengths and bead each strand.
6. Attach the silverware to the strands by looping the wire through the holes and attaching with a crimp.
7. Thread the ends of the silverware strands through the holes at the bottom of the teapot and affix with crimps or end pieces.
8. Thread the ends of the top strands through the top holes of the teapot for hanging. Affix with crimps or end pieces as desired.
9. Hold the top strands together for hanging with the fishing tackle parts. Thread the wire through the crimp, add the snap swivel and then carefully push the wire back through the crimp and close with pliers.

SOLAR-POWERED FOUNTAIN & PLANTER

Create your own solar-powered fountain and plater in less than an hour! The toughest part of this craft is picking the best location for the fountain, as it will work only when the sun is shining directly on the solar panels. Also, once assembled, the fountain will be difficult to move. Once you nail down a location nailed down and do a bit of shopping at the garden center, it will come together quickly and easily.

MATERIALS
- **2-3 pots of different sizes (1 pot must be able to nest inside a larger pot)**
- **Platform to go in larger pot**
- **Potting soil**
- **Plants**
- **Solar-powered fountain unit**

DIRECTIONS

1. If your smaller container has drainage holes, you'll need to plug them, as it will hold the water for the fountain. Try cork to plug the holes and then cover the bottom of the pot with heavy-duty plastic using hot glue. (You don't have to use cork, but choose a material that won't deteriorate under water.) Make sure all the edges of the plastic are glued down and everything is dry. To check for leaks, pour a pitcher of water into the pot. If the large pot doesn't have drainage holes, carefully drill a few in the bottom.

2. Place the platform insert into the larger pot. Set the smaller pot firmly on the platform insert. Make sure it's level and secure. Fill the space between the pots with potting soil.

3. Slowly add water to the smaller pot, making sure the pot stays level and safely seated in the soil. When the small pot is full, plant the flowers or greenery in the large pot and pack the soil tightly around the small pot to keep it secure. Water the plants until the water seeps out the drainage hole of the bottom pot, adding soil to the pot as necessary.

4. Assemble the solar fountain per manufacturer's directions. Place fountain in water per package directions.

5. Once the water begins to circulate through the fountain, add water to the small container as needed.

6. If applicable, carefully drill drainage holes in bottom of third container. Set third container near fountain as desired. Fill with soil and plants.

HANDMADE HELPER
When it comes to upcycling, anything is fair game! Red wagons, rusty wheelbarrows and old washtubs make great containers for fountains. (Be sure to add drainage holes.) For the dragonfly craft, scout garage sales and thrift shops for old baking pans and weathered pieces of sheet metal.

CRAFT: VICKI SCHILLEMAN

• • •

LICENSE PLATE DRAGONFLY

Here's a great way to give new life to discarded items. Hang the dragonfly on a tree or fence, or use it indoors for a rustic and unique wall hanging. Get creative with paint colors for the body and materials for making the antennae and tail. And get the kids involved! They can paint the body, name the dragonfly and help find a place to hang it.

MATERIALS

- Paint
- 1 chair leg or spindle
- 4 license plates
- Old keys, 1 key ring, heavy-gauge wire (or other decorations)
- Seven 1-in. multipurpose screws (or more as needed)
- Picture hanger
- Marker
- Safety gloves
- Metal file
- All-purpose aviation snips or cutting torch (see note)
- Drill

DIRECTIONS

1. Paint the chair leg in a color that coordinates with the license plates.
2. Create a pattern for the dragonfly's wings. The craft in the photo below has 9½x4-in. wings. Trace the pattern onto the underside of each license plate. Trace 2 for the left side, flip the pattern and trace 2 for the right side.
3. Wearing heavy gloves to protect your hands, use snips to cut out the wing pieces along the pattern lines. File down rough edges.
4. Lay out the pieces, right sides up, as you want them to look when attached to the chair leg (body). On the wrong sides, mark the top-right (TR), bottom-right (BR), top-left (TL) and bottom-left (BL) pieces.
5. With the wrong sides up, position the top-right piece (TR) beside the top-left piece (TL) on the body, overlapping slightly to form the upper set of wings. Drill 2 holes through both plates into the body. Repeat for the bottom set of wings.
6. Attach the wings to the body, using 4 screws.
7. Use remaining screws to attach keys or other decorations to your dragonfly. (The photo below has keys at the head and eyes, and antennae of heavy-gauge wire drilled into the top.) Attach a key ring with key to the bottom to decorate the tail.
8. Attach a picture hanger to the underside to hang the dragonfly.

NOTE: Aviation snips are sold at home improvement stores. Certain license plates may require a stronger tool, such as a cutting torch. Be sure to wear safety gear.

DIY SPOON RAIN CHAIN

Think gutters are ugly? Rain chains are a beautiful way to harness the power of water. The concept is simple: Surface tension and gravity guide the water down a chain. Now you can create your own rustic water feature for only a few dollars using salvaged spoons. If you are looking for spoons at the thrift store, be sure to select thinner ones so they will be easy to bend and drill, and choose a wire that is rustproof and simple to manipulate.

MATERIALS
- **Spoons**
- **Wire**
- **Drill**
- **Sharp drill bit**
- **Needle-nose pliers**
- **Bench vise or clamp and pliers**

DIRECTIONS

1. Decide how long you want the rain chain to be.

2. Using a bench vise, bend enough spoons to complete the project. If you don't have a vise, use a hand clamp to secure the flat part of the spoon against a table with the rest of it hanging over. Use pliers to bend the spoon downward.

3. Remove the bowls from about a dozen spoons. Use the same method as in Step 2, but keep bending each spoon back and forth until the bowl snaps off.

4. Carefully drill holes in end of each spoon handle, including the handles without bowls.

5. Put 2 spoons together back to back so bowls face outward. Fit a bowl-less handle between the handles of the 2 spoons, leaving several inches extended past the spoons (see photo at right). The protruding end of the handle should have the hole in it.

6. Wrap wire around all 3 handles just above the bowls.

7. Wire together the handles of the spoons at the opposite end as tightly as you can. Be sure to leave some extra wire for attaching the next segment. Repeat this step until you have used all of the spoons.

8. Once all the segments are assembled, attach them to each other by twisting together the extra wire you left at both ends. Make sure to leave enough wire on the top end of your chain for hanging.

9. Hang the rain chain from a tree limb above a garden, or use it in place of a downspout above a splash block to direct water away from the house. Or, set a decorative glazed pot or rain barrel below the chain to collect the rain water if desired.

BIRDBATH MINI GARDEN

Transform an old birdbath into a tiny landscape with this easy idea. Add a little magic with a stone pathway or a few fairy garden accents.

MATERIALS
- **Old birdbath or other container**
- **Bagged potting mix**
- **Planting material (see Miniature Plant Picks at right)**
- **Small stones, gravel or pine bark nuggets**
- **Fairy garden accessories, optional**

DIRECTIONS

1. Before planting, place a birdbath or other container, such as a terra-cotta pot or wooden box, where it will stay permanently. (It will be too heavy to move later.)

2. Play around with the landscape design with the plants still in their pots to make things easier on yourself and the plants.

3. Fill the planter about two-thirds full with the potting mix.

4. Remove 1 plant at a time from pots. Position the plants in the potting mix by spreading the roots of each as widely as you can, leaving room for neighboring plants. (This step is especially important if you are using a birdbath or similarly shallow planter.)

5. Once you are satisfied with the arrangement, add as much potting mix as possible to cover the roots, but not so much that watering will wash it away. Gently water all plants.

6. If desired, add decorative accessories and features.

NOTE: When creating your mini garden, try using everyday items in a new way: Gravel can be a tiny stone path; tumbled glass transforms into a shimmering pond. Fairy garden decorations, sold online or at craft stores, range from minuscule arbors and bridges to tiny houses and animal figurines. Just one will lend a lovely scale and bit of flair to your miniature birdbath garden.

MINIATURE PLANT PICKS

Not sure where to start? Give these a try!

SUCCULENTS
Use them for accent plants or "shrubs."
- Stonecrop sedum
- Limelight sedum
- Blue Spruce sedum
- Silver Onion echeveria
- Hen-and-chicks

GROUND COVERS
Create a mat of green in the miniature garden, and a "waterfall" over the planter.
- Golden club moss (*Selaginella kraussiana* 'Aurea')
- Scotch moss (*Sagina subulata* 'Aurea')
- Blue Star creeper
- Pink cranesbill (*Erodium* x *variabile* 'Bishop's Form')

CONIFERS
Provide woodland "shade" and a layer of realism.
- Jervis dwarf Canadian hemlock
- Dwarf Pagoda Japanese holly
- Mont Bruno boxwood
- Fernspray false cypress
- Lime Glow juniper

CRAFTS (2): ALISON AUTH; PHOTOS: HEIDI HESS

STEPPING-STONE PATH

Stepping-stone paths offer many of the advantages of concrete sidewalks and paver stone but without all the work, expense and mess. You can save wear and tear on your lawn in heavily used routes, take a trip to the garden without getting your feet wet from the morning dew, and add a touch of elegance to an otherwise plain expanse of lawn. Since you only remove enough sod to place the stones, you can lay this path without tearing up your yard. And if you pile the dirt and sod on a tarp as you work, cleanup can be easy as well.

Almost any type of flat stones will work as long as they're about 2 in. thick. You can often pick up limestone stepping-stones at local landscape supply centers for as little as $2 each. You'll also need a 60-pound bag of playground sand for every 10 stones.

MATERIALS
- **Limestone stepping stones**
- **Gardening trowel**
- **Drywall keyhole saw**
- **Playground sand**

DIRECTIONS
1. Space the stepping-stones along the path to match your stride. Using the stones as patterns, cut through the sod around each stone with a drywall saw or a bread knife (Photo 1).
2. Move the stone to the side and dig out the sod with a trowel (Photo 2). Dig the hole 1 in. deeper than the thickness of the stone to allow for the sand base.
3. Roughly level a 1-in. layer of sand in the hole (Photo 3). Set the stone over the sand and wiggle it until the stone is flush with the surrounding sod. Add or remove sand as necessary.

PHOTO 1

PHOTO 2

PHOTO 3

WATERFALL WIND CHIMES

Liven up your backyard when you reuse tin cans to make these dazzling wind chimes. It's a fairly simple craft to construct, marking it a perfect way to spend an afternoon or create something special with the family. Best of all, it is customizable. You can make large or tiny wind chimes, paint the cans your favorite color, or add some glitter or sequins for a little sparkle. Start planning meals that use up the canned goods in your pantry, and create these fun wind chimes soon!

MATERIALS

- Fishing line
- Split shot fishing weights
- Cans, 3 different sizes
- Finishing nail
- Hammer
- Needle-nose pliers
- Baubles, beads, etc.
- Wire
- Old lampshade

DIRECTIONS

1. Carefully punch a hole in the center of the can bottoms with the finishing nail and hammer.
2. Take a length of fishing line long enough to attach 3 cans with room at the top for hanging, and attach a bauble at one end with either a knot or a split shot.
3. Using the pliers, squeeze a split shot onto the line roughly 6 to 7 in. above the bauble.
4. Thread the line through the smallest can. Add another split shot a few inches above the small can. Next, thread the medium-size can onto the line. Place it so the small can hangs inside the medium one, and squeeze the split shot tight. Repeat, adding the largest can to the top of the line.
5. Continue making lines of cans until you have as many as you want, varying the spacing of the cans along each line. (The wind chimes pictured at right have 7 sets of cans, or 21 total cans.)
6. Use the round upper frame of the lamp shade for the wind chime's hanger. In the center of the round frame, attach a wire or another piece of a lamp frame (as we did here) for easy hanging.

7. Arrange the cans on a table in the pattern you want them to hang.
8. Attach the cans by looping each line over the frame and squeezing a split shot tight with pliers. Be sure the loop is snug but not too tight around the frame's wire.
9. Trim any excess fishing line, and hang the wind chimes.

WIND CHIME: CRAFT, ALISON AUTH; PHOTO, HEIDI HESS; FENCE ART: JOANNE KENNEY

HANDMADE HELPER
Old chandelier teardrops make perfect baubles for the wind chimes, but also try beads or anything that dangles. If you want to add even more pizazz, make some extra strings of baubles and attach them to the chimes as well.

FENCE ART

Beautify a simple open fence with a fanciful, free-form design made of plastic tablecloths. From dragonflies to dragons, any design works! Get creative and let your imagination take over.

MATERIALS
○ **Plastic tablecloths in multiple colors**
○ **Scissors**

DIRECTIONS
1. Cut plastic tablecloths into long strips.
2. Weave one color of plastic strips in and out of the fence openings to create a design outline. Tie the ends of the strips to the fence to secure.
3. Weave other colors inside the outline to completely fill it in, tying off and tucking the ends of the strips back in on themselves to secure.

BOWLING BALL BUGS

Retiring an old bowling ball? Create a striking ladybug for any garden—big or small. These garden pets are as easy as 1-2-3, so they're a great project for kids to help with.

A quart is the smallest can of mixed paint you can buy at the hardware store, but smaller quantities of acrylic hobby paint are available at craft stores. If you do have extra, use it to make a colony of bugs—or gifts for your envious neighbors! These cute critters also make perfect housewarming gifts and change-of-pace donations at charity raffles.

MATERIALS

- **Bowling ball**
- **Black silicone caulk**
- **Two 8½-in. lengths of #6 copper wire (have the hardware store cut it for you)**
- **Two 1-in. round wooden beads**
- **1 qt. Kilz exterior primer**
- **1 qt. red exterior latex paint**
- **1 qt. black exterior latex paint**
- **Painter's tape**
- **Utility knife or scissors**
- **Stenciling brush or sponge**

DIRECTIONS

1. Prime and paint the bowling ball. Add coats as needed. After paint is completely dry, apply painter's tape in the desired pattern. Stipple on black paint with a stenciling brush or sponge for texture (Photo 1).

2. Make your own stencil by cutting different-sized circles from 2 pieces of painter's tape put edge to edge. We used 2½-in.- and 1¾-in.-diameter dots. Stipple the dots. Carefully remove the paint once the paint dries completely (Photo 2).

3. Paint wooden beads with the black paint. Once dry, affix to copper wires with black caulk.

4. Fill bowling ball thumb hole with black caulk. Set in the 2 antennae (Photo 3). Prop antennae up so they don't droop while drying. Let dry for at least 24 hours.

PHOTO 1

PHOTO 2

PHOTO 3

KEEP YOUR CRITTER COMPANY

Is your ladybug lonely? Craft a bumblebee to add to the garden. To make a bee, simply paint stripes with yellow and black paint. Next, add wings made of copper wire and hardware cloth.

GLASS IN THE GARDEN

Turn mismatched plates, bowls or candleholders into beautiful, show-stopping glass flowers and add a splash of color to your backyard decor. Use any style of glass plates or bowls you have on hand and paint them any colors you want. Best of all, this kind of flower requires no watering!

While the directions below are for 1 flower, they look best in small groups of 3 or 4. Gather up several glass plates, bowls and candleholders the next time you're at a rummage sale, flea market or secondhand store.

MATERIALS

- 3 glass plates, bowls or dishes in different sizes
- 1 glass candleholder, salt or pepper shaker, or small vase (for center of flower)
- 1 small vase with at least one flat side
- Alcohol wipes
- Glass paint
- Paintbrushes or sponges
- Markers or pens for glass
- Clear, waterproof silicone
- Metal or PVC pipe

DIRECTIONS

1. Clean all glass thoroughly with alcohol wipes and let it dry.

2. Use a sponge or paintbrush to paint the glass pieces, covering completely. Add details like stripes, circles or petals if desired. A couple of layers might be necessary to get full coverage. Use markers or pens to add small details.

3. Bake the glass pieces according to the directions on the paint bottles. (In general, bake at 325° on the top rack for about 20 minutes.) Turn off the oven, and let the glass pieces cool completely before removing them.

4. Lay the largest plate flat on a covered surface. Apply silicone to the bottom of the next largest piece and press it down onto your base plate.

5. Continue applying silicone to the bottom of each of the smaller pieces until the flower is assembled. Let the entire piece dry overnight.

6. Apply silicone to a flat side of the small vase and, holding the vase upside down, press it to the back of the flower. This will serve as the mount that fits over the pipe

for display purposes. Let the silicone dry overnight.

7. Pound the pipe into the ground; slip the flower over the pipe.

NOTE: Avoid using very thin glass plates as they can break in the oven while baking. Open windows or turn on the exhaust fan while plates are baking as some paints might give off a strong odor when baking.

INSIDE-OUTSIDE CHANDELIER

Give an old indoor light fixture new life in the garden with the power of the sun.

MATERIALS

- Chandelier
- Solar lights on stakes
- Painter's tape
- Weather-resistant spray paint with primer
- Screwdriver
- Wire cutters
- Industrial glue

DIRECTIONS

1. Clean chandelier if needed. Remove old lights, candles and wiring with a screwdriver and wire cutters, leaving the flat base on each arm.

2. Separate the solar light fixtures from the stakes. Set the stakes aside. Separate the glass or plastic sconces of light fixtures from the solar tops and bases. Move the sconces away from work area to protect from spray paint.

3. Tape over the solar panels on lights. Spray-paint the chandelier, light tops and bases. Dry completely.

4. Remove tape and reassemble solar lights. Using industrial glue, attach lights to the bases of chandelier.

5. Hang finished chandelier.

FANTASTIC FLIERS

Let your imagination take wing with a bit of copper wire and some beads. This project captures the delicacy and colors of butterflies and dragonflies in simple garden ornaments. Older kids might enjoy making these attractive insects, and younger children can help pick out the beads.

A rod inserted in the back of your creation helps you set it in the ground for a hovering effect. Or, leave the rod off and hang the craft on a fence or the front door for a fun and dazzling display.

The following directions help you craft a dragonfly, but once you get the basics down, it's easy to create butterflies, bees, birds and other favorite fliers.

MATERIALS

- ⅜-in. (outside diameter) flexible copper tubing
- 1/16 x36-in. brass rod (1 length for each dragonfly)
- ⅛ x36-in. brass rod (support)
- 20-gauge copper wire (1 roll)
- 9/32 in.-diameter spring about 1½ in. long
- Rosin-core leaded solder (for electrical and hobby work)
- Glass beads
- 6-in. wood dowel
- Superglue gel or quick-setting epoxy

TOOLS

- Wire cutters
- Needle-nose pliers
- Tube cutter or hacksaw
- Power drill and drill bits (1/16 in. and ⅛ in.)
- ¾-in. spade bit
- Mini torch or soldering iron
- Fine steel wool

BODY

Cut copper tubing to 4 in. with a tubing cutter or hacksaw. Make slight indentations in the copper at the hole locations (see Figure A at far right), using an awl or sharp drywall screw so the drill bit does not slip off when you begin drilling.

Drill holes for the wings and eyes with the 1/16-in. bit. Drill a ⅛-in. hole in the bottom for the support rod. Drill the eye holes from both sides rather than straight through so the eyes will be aligned.

Cut a 3-ft. length of 1/16-in. brass rod in half and clean the rods and the body tube with steel wool.

Push both rods through the middle holes and center them. Apply just enough heat to melt the solder. Touch the solder to the heated metal (not the flame). Solder to the underbelly with 1 drop of solder (Photo 1).

PHOTO 1

PHOTO 2

PHOTO 3

WINGS

Make a jig to form the wings on a scrap piece of ¾-in. wood. Drill holes, then glue and insert dowels (Photo 2). Mark the center, placing the body of the dragonfly between the 2 dowels, then bend 1 rod around the dowels for wings. Trim the ends so they meet back in the center of the dragonfly. Insert them into the proper holes in the body and solder in place.

BEADS AND EYES

Wrap about 24 in. of 20-gauge copper wire around the ⅜-in. copper tubing, then stretch it out (Photo 3) and cut it in half.

Twist 1 end around the tip of a wing and solder it. Thread on the glass beads, then attach the other end and solder or superglue the wire where it crosses the body. Glue beads in place.

Insert a 6-in. length of 20-gauge wire through the eye holes. Slide on 2 eye beads, cross the wires and wrap them once around the body. Bend excess wire into legs and solder the wire at the bottom.

Attach the spring into the back end of the dragonfly with superglue or quick-setting epoxy. If you can't find this size spring, make your own by coiling 20-gauge copper wire around a ¼-in. machine bolt.

Solder the ⅛-in. brass rod in the hole on the bottom side of the body. Push the rod into the ground and watch your dragonfly hover all year long.

> **HANDMADE HELPER**
> Remember to test your beads first. Not all beads you may want to use will fit onto the wings' twisty wires.

FIGURE A
COPPER TUBE HOLE LOCATIONS

Drill ¹⁄₁₆-in. holes through both sides of the tube. Drill a ⅛-in. bottom support hole (not shown) only halfway through.

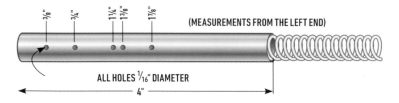

⅜" ¾" 1¼" 1⅜" 1⅞"

(MEASUREMENTS FROM THE LEFT END)

ALL HOLES ¹⁄₁₆" DIAMETER

4"

STARS AT NIGHT

These patriotic luminaries are nearly as much fun as Fourth of July fireworks.

MATERIALS

- 3 jar lids with wire hangers
- Spray paint, optional
- 3 qt.-sized Mason jars
- Star stickers or a star template and adhesive sheet
- Red, white and blue acrylic craft paint
- Decoupage glue
- 3 tea lights or three strings of battery-operated mini lights
- Small paintbrush

DIRECTIONS

1. Spray-paint lids, if desired. Dry thoroughly.

2. Using template, if needed, cut out star stickers from adhesive sheet. Cover jars in a decorative pattern with stickers.

3. Paint 1 jar red, 1 white and 1 blue with acrylic paint. Dry thoroughly. Repeat with a second coat of paint.

4. Carefully remove stickers. Touch up paint as needed and dry thoroughly.

5. Paint a coat of decoupage glue over each jar and dry thoroughly.

6. Insert lights into jars. Top with lids.

ALL WRAPPED UP

Yarn globes make creative shades for a simple string of lights. Chose yarn in coordinating colors to add instant flair.

MATERIALS

- Yardstick or clothes drying rack
- Sheet of plastic
- Round balloons
- String
- 8 oz. all-purpose craft glue
- Plastic bowl
- Craft stick
- Multicolored yarn
- String of lights
- Clear fishing line
- Tweezers

DIRECTIONS

1. Prepare a place to hang globes to dry. A yardstick balanced across two chairs works well, as does a clothes drying rack. Cover the floor with plastic.

2. Blow up balloons to about a 4-in. diameter and tie off, inflating 1 or 2 more than desired number of finished globes, in case of breakage. Tie a string around the end of each to hang.

3. Squeeze glue into a plastic bowl. Add 2 oz. water and stir with a craft stick.

4. Cut long pieces of yarn, keeping length manageable to work with. Dip 1 piece of yarn in glue mixture and wrap strand around a balloon in a random pattern, squeezing the excess glue out as you work. Wrap strand as desired, cutting excess yarn at the end. Tuck the end under another strand to secure. Leave at least 1 opening in the pattern wide enough to fit a bulb on the string of lights.

5. Hang globe in prepared area. The glue should not drip; if it does, add more glue to the bowl before working on the next balloon. Repeat process for remaining balloons, alternating yarn colors as desired. Dry globes for 24 hours.

6. Pop balloons and carefully remove with tweezers. Remove any excess dried glue from the globes.

7. Slide a bulb from light string into each globe. Secure globes to light string with fishing line.

CRAFTS: SAMANTHA BENDER (2)

STRIKING YARD ART

Get those old bowling balls out of the gutter and gussy them up! With a little work, they make the perfect garden decor...and hardly cost a thing. Cover the ball as you see fit, using river rocks, glass gems or ceramic or mirrored tiles.

MATERIALS

- Bowling ball
- Silicone caulk
- Tile adhesive
- Polished river rocks, glass gems or mirrored tile
- Grout (any color)
- Acrylic grout additive
- Putty knife
- Sponge

DIRECTIONS

1. Fill the bowling balls' finger holes with silicone caulk.

2. Spread adhesive on the bowling ball with a putty knife and place rocks onto the adhesive, leaving ½ in. between the rocks for easy grouting. (Depending on where you plan to display your piece, you might want to leave an area on the bottom of the ball open to provide the best balance.) Let dry for 24 hours.

3. Mix the grout, using grout additive, to the consistency of a thick cake mix. Apply the grout with a sponge, wiping off any excess, and let it dry.

4. Place the ball on a gazing-ball stand or directly in garden as desired.

HANDMADE HELPER
When creating the glass-gem ball (below), use silicone caulk instead of grout and pack the gems tightly. The caulk oozes out for a smoother look. When creating the other varieties, use grout additive instead of water; it will allow the grout to weather better.

GLASS GEMS

MIRRORED TILES

CERAMIC TILE

RIVER ROCK

CRAFT: LYNNE HANSEN

PRETTY PLANT MARKERS

Your favorite plants deserve more recognition than a simple stick with black ink spelling out its name. Try making these unique plant markers, which hold a label or a seed packet with bent copper wire easily set in a decorative base.

These are so basic to assemble, you can really let your creativity flow. Decorate the cement base with rocks, glass beads or even seashells. They're great gifts for friends and relatives. Create a few hostess gifts for housewarming parties, backyard get-togethers and other events for the gardeners in your life.

MATERIALS

- ○ **Copper wire or ¼-in. flexible copper tubing**
- ○ **12/2 electrical cable, plastic sheathing stripped off wires**
- ○ Small trowel
- ○ 1 bag premixed mortar (60 lb.)
- ○ Rocks, glass beads, seashells
- ○ 2-gal. bucket
- ○ 4x8x2-in. disposable plastic container
- ○ Wooden spoon
- ○ Nonstick cooking spray
- ○ Dowel
- ○ Wire cutters
- ○ Dust mask

DIRECTIONS

1. Hold a dowel 8 in. up from the end of a 5-ft. piece of wire folded in half. Wrap the wire around, forming a loop (Photo 1). Move the dowel over 3½ in. or the width

Quarter-inch flexible copper tubing and glass beads.

Copper flashing with the plant name written with permanent marker.

Braided copper wire seed packet holder.

PHOTO 1

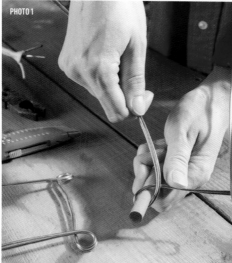

PHOTO 2

PHOTO 3

needed to fit your seed packet and wrap it again, making a second loop in the opposite direction. Cut the wire off even with the first leg. Bend a ½-in. 90° turn at the bottom of each leg to help anchor it in the mortar.

2. Wearing a dust mask, use a wooden spoon to thoroughly mix the mortar in the bucket to the consistency of cookie dough. Slowly add water to the dry mix as needed. Let sit for about 3 minutes, then remix, adding a dash more water if needed. Coat the plastic container with cooking spray. Fill the container. Give the container a few quick shakes to settle the mortar. Then, using a small trowel (Photo 2), form a mound of mortar on top so the mortar resembles a loaf of baked bread. Gently push the copper marker into the mortar so the 90° bends are about ½ in. up from the bottom and centered. If the mortar is too wet to support the wire,

let it stiffen up a little before trying again.

3. Starting at the edges of the base and working your way toward the center, arrange the rocks, beads or shells to your liking. Embed the decorations at least halfway into the mortar. If you don't like how a rock looks, remove it quickly, rinse it off and reposition.

4. Let completed marker set for at least 24 hours before removing it from the plastic container.

HANDMADE HELPER
We added a latex bonding agent to the mortar. It's not necessary, but it'll make the mortar stick better to smooth rocks.

Make an
ENTRANCE

WARM WELCOME MAT

Want a simple way to add personality to your front door? Try the oh-so-easy technique of reverse stenciling—essentially, blocking out where you don't want paint—on an outdoor mat. Cardboard, scissors and spray paint are all you need!

MATERIALS

- **Jute or coir doormat**
- **Cardboard**
- **Scissors**
- **Enamel spray paint**

DIRECTIONS

1. Make the address stencils by printing numbers 4 to 6 in. high from your computer; trace onto the cardboard and cut out with scissors. (Or buy wooden numbers from a craft store.) To make the cardboard circles, trace around jars, bowls, lids, etc., of different sizes.
2. Pin stencils to the mat and place on a drop cloth in a well-ventilated area.
3. Spray with enamel paint in a circular motion until all areas are evenly covered. Let dry for 2 hours, and then apply a second coat. In another 2 hours, remove the stencils carefully to avoid smudging the edges.

HANDMADE HELPER
Coir mats are made from the husk and shell of coconuts—materials that were once considered waste. Today, eco-conscious textile designers use coir in lots of clever applications.

UPCYCLED ARBOR

Nothing says "welcome" like an old-fashioned arbor covered in your favorite vine or climber. All you need are old ladders and a handful of screws to transform an existing gate into a grand entryway and add some drama to your yard.

MATERIALS

- **3 wooden ladder sections (stepladders, extension ladders or library ladders)**
- **2-in. wood or drywall screws**
- **Screw gun or screwdriver**
- **Drill and drill bit**
- **Sandpaper, rough or medium and fine grit**
- **Palm sander, optional**
- **Exterior-grade primer**
- **Exterior-grade paint**
- **Stiff wire, optional**

DIRECTIONS

1. If you're using extension ladders or stepladders, separate them into individual sections. The upright or supporting ladders should each be at least 7 ft. before mounting; the overhead ladder can be shorter, depending on the width of your gate.
2. Lay out ladder sections on the ground before you cut them to size. Make sure the rungs of the overhead ladder won't interfere with mounting to the uprights. Once you have lined up the pieces, mark the edges where the overhead ladder should be cut, if necessary, leaving an overhang of 5-6 in. on each end.
3. Trim both the supporting ladders to the same height, unless you must accommodate a steep grade at the site.
4. Sand the ladder sections, first with rough- or medium-grit sandpaper and then with fine-grit for a smooth finish. Prime and paint the ladders. Allow paint to dry thoroughly.
5. Position one of the uprights against a front gatepost. You may need to excavate ground at the base so the ladder stands level and is well supported. Drill pilot holes (slightly smaller than the screw width) through the ladder piece and into the post. The example shown at right used 4 screws per ladder, 2 at the lower end and 2 at the top end of the gatepost. Attach ladder to post with the screws. Repeat for the second upright on the opposite gatepost.
6. Lay third ladder over the 2 uprights. Ours was wider than the supporting ladders so it slid right over them. Bend S-shaped hooks out of rigid wire to hold it at each end. If the overhead ladder is the same width as the uprights, place 1 side along the outside front of 1 upright and the other end of the same side along the inside front of the other upright so the overhead rests on the uprights' rungs. Screw pieces together where they meet, drilling pilot holes first.
7. Choose a vining plant for your arbor. We chose Carolina jasmine (*Gelsemium sempervirens*), which produces profuse yellow blooms in spring. This plant also is evergreen, a rapid grower, lightweight and noninvasive.

PHOTO 1

PHOTO 2

PHOTO 3

RUSTIC WINDOW BOX

A window box should be as pretty as the plants that go inside. This project will make an attractive place to grow herbs for snipping and cooking. Scalloped lead sheeting dabbed with white vinegar gives your box a rustic, mottled look.

MATERIALS

- **Plain window box (either buy one or make your own)**
- **Roll of lead flashing (sold at roofing supply stores or online)**
- **Length of 1×1-in. softwood batten**
- **1¼-in. deck screws**
- **Galvanized ¾-in. roofing nails**
- **Tin snips**
- **Drill**
- **Hammer**
- **White vinegar**
- **Herbs or flowers in clay pots**
- **Brackets to hang window box, optional**

DIRECTIONS

1. Measure the height of the box and the length of the front plus the 2 sides; you don't need to cover the back unless it will be visible. Use tin snips to cut a strip of lead a little longer than this so you can bend the surplus behind to make neat corners. Flatten the lead onto the box, using a small flat piece of wood and a hammer, and nail it in place.

2. Cut 3 lengths of batten, 2 for the sides and 1 for the front. The scalloped frill will be fixed to these pieces. Fix the battens around the top of the box. Drill holes through the box from inside and drive screws through the holes into the battens.

3. Cut the scalloped trim and nail to the top of the front batten (Photo 1).

4. Snip notches out at the corners and bend scalloped edge down (Photo 2). Bend the strip around the corners and fold it over the top edges of the side battens. Tap smoothly into place, using a piece of wood and a hammer. Fix in place with nails driven into tops of battens.

5. For a weathered patina, dab white vinegar onto the surface with a cloth until you get a mottled effect (Photo 3). Paint the inside of the box if desired. Mount with brackets if desired.

WORKING WITH LEAD

- Use a large nail and a straightedge to score straight cutting lines in lead.
- For the scalloped edge, use a can or jelly jar as a template and mark the cutting line with a nail.
- Wear gloves to protect your hands.
- Lead is toxic—wash your hands after handling it!

BEE OUR GUEST

A honeycomb wreath offers a sweet welcome to family and friends.

MATERIALS

- Oval frame
- Foam core board with adhesive
- Yellow burlap fabric
- Chicken wire
- Utility or fabric tape
- Fabric flowers of various sizes
- Clothespins
- Decorative cardstock of your choice
- Utility knife
- Hot glue gun
- Wire cutters

DIRECTIONS

1. Remove back and glass from frame. Trace frame opening on foam core board. Using utility knife, cut foam core to fit into frame.

2. Cut burlap a few inches larger than foam core. Remove adhesive backing from foam and place fabric right side up on adhesive. Press into place, removing wrinkles. Flip over and trim excess fabric. Hot-glue edge of fabric to back of foam.

3. Using wire cutters, cut chicken wire slightly larger than the foam core. Place on top of burlap. Gently pull chicken wire around the back. Using utility or fabric tape, carefully tape down the excess chicken wire.

4. Hot-glue larger fabric flowers to the frame edge. Hot-glue smaller flowers to clothespins and arrange on chicken wire. Attach card stock with a clothespin.

CAN BOO!

Light an October night with these spooktacular luminaries.

MATERIALS

- 3 clean tin cans
- Black spray paint made for metal
- Orange grease marker
- 1 spring clamp
- Drill with metal drill bit or a nail, a block of wood and a hammer
- Orange tissue paper
- Black tape
- Small battery-operated candles

DIRECTIONS

1. Coat the insides and outsides of the cans with spray paint. Use several sheer coats of paint for even coverage.

2. With the grease marker, make dots that form one letter of the word "BOO" on each can. Placing the dots in the valleys of the cans' ridges makes drilling or hammering easier.

3. Clamp the can to a table; use the drill (or a hammer and nail with a block of wood inside the can) to punch holes.

4. Cut squares of tissue paper that are ½ in. larger than the punched letters; tape them inside the can behind the pierced holes of each letter.

5. Place small battery-operated candles inside the cans.

HERBAL WREATH

Create this beautiful living wreath in just three easy steps!

MATERIALS

- **Ready-made sphagnum peat moss wreath (preferably with a hanger attached)**
- **Basin or washtub**
- **Topiary pins**
- **Shears**
- **Assorted herbs or flowers (we used chives, purple basil, sweet basil, Cuban oregano, feverfew and tricolor sage)**

DIRECTIONS

1. Half-fill a large basin or tub with water and set it on a flat, sturdy surface. Dip the wreath inside and splash water on it. Let the wreath soak for a few seconds, until it's damp enough for planting. (To make your own wreath, buy sphagnum peat moss and pack it into a wire form. Then experiment with different shapes and sizes. Just make sure the hanging hardware supports the weight of the finished wreath.)

2. Before you begin planting, arrange the plants according to color and size around the wreath to get a good idea of the finished product. When you're satisfied, use your thumbs to make small holes where you can insert the plants. (In the wreath above, chives were planted first because they occupy the outermost edge. Bushier herbs, like basil and oregano, were added next.) Continue to add plants until your wreath is full.

STEP 1

STEP 2

STEP 3

3. Secure plants with topiary pins. The pins keep the plants in place and allow you to position foliage to help cover up bare spots. The plants grow while maintaining the shape of the wreath. Snip any unruly plants with shears, and hang your finished wreath on a wall or door. Planning to harvest fresh herbs from it regularly? Display it in the kitchen in a sunny spot.

• • •

ROPE THEM IN

Twist it, tie it and welcome guests to your home with this charming lariat.

MATERIALS

- **62 ft. of ½-in.-wide sisal twisted rope**
- **14-in.-wide wire wreath frame**
- **22-gauge floral wire**
- **Decorations of your choice**
- **Utility knife**
- **Wire cutters**
- **Hot glue gun**

DIRECTIONS

1. Use utility knife to cut four 1-yd. lengths of rope; set rope aside for Step 4.
2. Place wire wreath frame flat to work. Layer most of the remaining 50 ft. of rope in circular loops on top of frame.
3. With about 6 ft. of rope remaining, create a double hanging loop at top of wreath. Wrap remainder of rope tightly around itself and the wire frame backing. Secure hanging loop to back side with a clove hitch or simple knot. Apply hot glue to end of rope and knot to secure in place and prevent fraying.
4. In 4 symmetrically placed points on the wreath, wrap 1 of the remaining 1-yd. pieces tightly around the ropes and wire frame. (Use photo as a guide.) Secure each wrapped piece in place with a knot on the back side of the wreath. Use hot glue to prevent fraying.
5. Use a pair of wire cutters to cut several segments of floral wire. Attach layered strands of rope to wire frame using floral wire segments. Secure in at least 6 places around back of frame, making sure the rope does not sag.
6. Use hot glue to attach decorations such as silk flowers, mistletoe or freshly cut evergreen or holly branches.

NOTE: This weight of rope is easy to work with, but may sag if not fastened well to a strong wire wreath frame.

Pretty (Easy) PLANTERS

STEP 1

STEP 2

STEP 3

1-2-3 CONTAINER GARDEN

You are only three quick steps away from season-long blooms with this easy yet impressive container idea.

MATERIALS

- Potted plants
- Potting soil
- Plant pot or stand
- Basket with side planting holes

DIRECTIONS

1. Set the basket in the plant pot or stand. Decide which plant will serve as the center plant—the tall plant set in the middle of the arrangement.

2. Choose smaller edge plants with root balls of 3-4½ in. to place around the center plant.

3. Using potting soil, plant the edge plants in the side planting holes of the basket; alternate the types of edge plants. Using additional potting soil, plant the center plant in the basket.

NOTE: Start by choosing the plant that will be in the middle of your arrangement since it will be the focal point. Remember that it should be taller than the other plants, with texture and/or color that sets it apart from the other plants in the arrangement. Materials for this craft available at www.kinsmangarden.com.

TOP PICKS

Consider these options when selecting your center plant:

- Caladiums
- Blue salvia
- Giant coleus
- Grasses
- Pentas
- Persian shield

SITTING PRETTY PLANTER

A classic farmhouse spindle-back chair is the perfect seat for a lush fern, but feel free to refurbish any wooden chair into this pretty planter. Set it by the front door as a seasonal welcome for guests, as a focal point in your foyer, or on your summer porch for cottage charm. It won't stain your floor or deck, and it's the perfect height for tending.

MATERIALS

- **Chair**
- **Potted plant**
- **String and pencil**
- **Drill and large drill bit**
- **Jigsaw or small handsaw with fine teeth**
- **Paint scraper or putty knife , optional**
- **Sandpaper, rough and fine (100-200 grit)**
- **Orbital or palm sander , optional**
- **Enamel-based spray primer and spray paint**

DIRECTIONS

1. Measure the circumference of the pot based on where it will rest in the chair. Measure the circumference of the largest part of the pot to make sure it won't hit the back of the chair.

2. Mark the center point of the chair seat by measuring both the width and the depth of the seat, and mark the center of each. The point at which they intersect is the center of the seat.

3. Divide the diameter of desired hole size in half. Cut a piece of string several inches longer than that measurement. Tie a pencil to the string so that, with the string fully extended, it's half the diameter of the desired hole. Place the cut end of the string on your center mark and extend the pencil outward, carefully drawing a circle.

4. With the hole drawn, take a large drill bit and drill 1 or a series of contiguous holes just on the inside of your pencil line. The hole(s) must be large enough for a blade to fit through for sawing. Using a cutting tool of choice, cut along the circle drawn on the chair seat.

5. Depending on the condition of the chair, clean, scrape and sand it to prepare it for painting. For wooden chairs that haven't been painted or painted chairs with minimal wear, lightly sand the entire surface with fine-grit sandpaper to provide a "tooth," or bonding surface, for the primer.

6. Paint the chair. If the chair will be set outdoors, use enamel-based spray paint, which offer more protection than the latex varieties. Work outside or in a well-ventilated area. Use a gray or rust primer if the final paint color will be dark. If the final paint color will be bright, light or vibrant, use a white primer

7. Once the paint is dry, carefully insert the plant.

3-TIERED PORCH PLANTER

Give your porch a colorful face-lift with this project. It's a perfect way to put your house number, family name or the word "Welcome" on display for all to see. Buy precut outdoor vinyl numbers or letters at the craft or hardware store, then gather the supplies below and get started!

MATERIALS

- 5 round terra-cotta pots (8 in., 10 in., 12 in. and two 6 in.)
- Spray paint in your choice of 3 colors
- 4x2-in. (or slightly larger) outdoor vinyl house numbers or letters
- Potting soil and flowers
- Waterproof epoxy or outdoor glue, optional

DIRECTIONS

1. In a well-ventilated area, spray-paint the exterior of the 8-in., 10-in. and 12-in. pots in your choice of colors. Apply as many coats as needed, drying completely between coats, for full coverage. Let pots dry 24-48 hours.

2. Following manufacturer's instructions, carefully apply the vinyl numbers or the letters centered on 1 side of the 12-in. painted pot.

3. Decide where you'd like to set the completed planter and begin craft in that location. (Completed planter might be too heavy to move.) Put about 2 in. of potting soil in the 12-in. pot. Then place an unpainted 6-in. pot upside down, centered on the potting soil. Press the upside-down pot's rim into the soil to secure in place. Do the same, using more soil, inside the 10-in. pot with the remaining 6-in. pot. (The bottoms of these upside-down pots will provide a platform for the painted pots to sit on, forming tiers.)

4. Stack the 10-in. pot upside down inside the 12-in. pot, using the smaller pot as a base. Place the 8-in. pot inside the 10-in. pot in the same way. If desired, use a waterproof epoxy or outdoor glue to stabilize the pots.

5. Fill all 3 stacked pots with potting soil, stopping a few inches from the rims. (The soil should completely cover the upside-down pots, if possible.) Plant flowers as desired.

PERFECT FORM

Arrange your prettiest container yet using these three plant styles:

THRILLER

- Vertical accent in an arrangement is key. If the container will be visible from every angle, plant the thriller in the center. If the pot is placed against a wall, position the thriller in the back of the mix.

FILLER

- This type of plant has a mounding habit or is compact, anchoring the combo and filling in the gaps around neighboring plants. It should be planted in the middle ground of the pot, whether all the way around the thriller or front and center. Many designers use multiple fillers.

SPILLER

- A trailing plant that complements the thriller can make all the difference in a great container arrangement. Place one or more of this type close to the edges of the pot to drape over the container's sides. A spiller should be visible from all angles of the plant container.

STACKABLE GARDEN

Create a vertical blooming masterpiece when you give dresser drawers new life.

MATERIALS

- **Dresser drawers**
- **Handles**
- **Wood scraps**
- **Screws and screwdriver**
- **Power drill**
- **Sandpaper**
- **Exterior-grade paint and primer**
- **Plants**
- **Potting soil**
- **Finish nails, brads or staples, optional**
- **Lawn-and-leaf bags, optional**
- **House numbers , optional**

DIRECTIONS

1. Stack the drawers so they have a solid foundation and ample planting spaces. (We screwed together 2 matching drawers on the bottom to provide a wide, sturdy base. Next, we cantilevered all the boxes in opposite directions, using the center of the bottom 2 boxes as a visual guide.)

2. Once you know how you're going to arrange the drawers, make feet out of wood scraps and screw them onto the bottom drawer or drawers. (If using 2 drawers for the bottom, screw those together first, then attach the feet, including a fifth foot for support where the 2 base drawers meet.)

3. Next, drill about 10 drainage holes in the bottoms of all the drawers. The size of the hole is not critical; a drill bit of about ¼ in. should work fine.

4. Sand, prime and paint each drawer individually with exterior-grade coatings. You can paint the insides of the drawers as well, or you can shellac them to seal the wood to prevent decay. You can also leave the interiors unfinished and line them with plastic lawn-and-leaf bags if you prefer, but coating them in some way will definitely prolong their lifespan.

5. Experiment with the placement of the drawers. Attach any decorative handles, house numbers or other embellishments to the drawer faces.

6. Cut a piece of scrap wood the width of the bottom drawer to support the drawer above it. Secure the support board to the inside of the lower drawer with screws. Rest the next drawer on top of this support board and the perimeter of the drawer below and then secure it with screws, brads, pneumatic staples or finish nails. Repeat this process with all the drawers, working your way up from the bottom.

7. Cut at least 2 lengths of wood to the height of the finished unit (not including the legs); a 1x3-in. or 1x4-in. strip of wood is ideal. Screw these to the back of the unit, making sure to include each drawer. This provides rigid bracing and additional strength to the finished piece.

8. Set potted plants in the unit or take them out of the pots and plant directly in the drawers.

NOTE: Adding feet to this large planter ensures that water will drain freely away from the unit, preventing rot. Be sure the feet are chunky enough to support the weight of the unit.

• • •

INSTANT ANTIQUE POT

The attractive greenish cast that develops on old, weathered copper is called verdigris. A typical verdigris kit contains several small pots of paint, one for each layer, and a stippling brush. It can be used to transform wood, metal, plastic or terra-cotta containers.

MATERIALS
- **Terra-cotta pot**
- **Verdigris kit**
- **Stippling brush**
- **Paper towel**
- **Scrap paper**

DIRECTIONS

1. Wash your terra-cotta pot thoroughly and dry completely. Paint it all over with the first color in the kit. Dry completely.
2. Dip the stippling brush into the second, lighter paint color. Dab it on a piece of paper towel until it's almost dry. Then experiment by stippling some bits of scrap paper to achieve an even, light-colored impression.
3. Once you're happy with the effect, begin stippling the pot. You should end up with an almost transparent layer of paint through which the base coat can be seen. Repeat this process with each color supplied in the kit, ending with the metallic paint.

RETREAD & GROW

It's easy to put a fresh spin on a classic repurposed planter.

MATERIALS

- **Motorcycle or ATV tire**
- **Rust-Oleum Painter's Touch**
- **2x Ultra Cover spray paint**
- **Potting soil**
- **Flowers**
- **Power drill**
- **Heavy-duty rope**

DIRECTIONS

1. Drill drainage holes in the bottom of tire if needed.
2. Spray-paint tire, building up paint in layers over the span of an hour. Let dry completely.
3. Using the potting soil, plant seasonal flowers in the tire.
4. Wrap rope through tire and knot securely. Use rope to hang planter from a tree or porch.

NOTE: Used tires work better than new tires, which have a coating that can bleed through the paint. If using new tires, let dry for a couple of days after the first coat until the original tire color begins to show through, then add a fresh coat of paint.

> **HANDMADE HELPER**
> Keep the planter up all year. Simply replace the seasonal blooms with artificial foliage to easily add a bit of holiday flair to your yard.

CRAFT: STEPHANIE SLIWINSKI

KALEIDOSCOPE PLANTER

Recycle broken dishes or shattered bath tiles into works of garden art, like this colorful planter. Sure to brighten up any corner of your yard, it's easy and inexpensive to make. Just follow the simple instructions to create your own one-of-a-kind masterpiece.

MATERIALS

- **Terra-cotta pot**
- **Tile, smooth stones, glass beads and/or broken china**
- **Hammer**
- **Chalk**
- Nipper, optional
- **Polymer-fortified thin-set mortar**
- **Butter knife**
- **Sanded grout**
- **Gloves**
- **Wire brush**
- **Cloth**

DIRECTIONS

1. Wrap a tile in a cloth, glaze side down, and strike it with a hammer. Lay out the pieces on a flat surface to work out your design, and then chalk the design layout onto the pot. Shape the tile pieces with a nipper, if desired.

2. Mix a polymer-fortified thin-set mortar with water to the consistency of peanut butter. Using a butter knife, spread the mortar on the back of each tile and stick the tile on the pot, leaving a ¼-in. space between pieces for grout. Adhere the mosaic design pieces first and then fill in the background. Let set overnight.

3. Mix sanded grout with water to the consistency of peanut butter. Liberally slather the grout with gloved hand over the pot's surface, rubbing it into the spaces. Wipe excess off with a cloth.

4. Brush grout from the stones with a wire brush, then rub with a cloth to eliminate all brush marks.

STEP 1

STEP 2

STEP 3

Crafts for CRITTERS

A BIRD FOR THE BIRDS

This little birdhouse is simple, sweet and versatile. If you can find a box that matches the approximate size needed, then you'll be able to make this birdhouse almost before you can say "black-capped chickadee!"

MATERIALS

- 5-in. square box (built, reclaimed or purchased)
- Lauan for "bird" shape
- Small finish nails
- Picture-hanging hardware or wire and 2 screws
- 1-in. butt hinge
- Screen door hook and eye
- Glue
- Exterior latex primer and paint
- Shellac or other outdoor varnish
- Bird template
- Jigsaw
- Screw gun or drill
- 1¼-in. to 1½-in. hole saw
- Clamps
- Hammer
- Fine-grit sandpaper

DIRECTIONS

NOTE: If you are building the box, follow the instructions from step 1. If you already have a box, begin with step 6.

1. Cut one 5x5-in. square, two 5x4-¾-in. rectangles and two 4¾x4½-in. rectangles out of ¼-in. plywood, clear pine, shelf board, barn board or similar.

2. Glue one 5x4¾-in. rectangle to one 4¾x4½-in. rectangle. The 4¾-in. dimension is the height of both rectangles. Once joined, they will form an "L" with a short side and a longer side, but both will be the same height. Clamp until dry. Repeat with the other 2 rectangles.

3. Glue the two L-shaped side sections to the 5-in. square box bottom. Make sure the sections come together to form a perfect square. Clamp until dry.

4. Once dry, reinforce the joints with small finish nails or brads.

5. Sand box with fine-grit sandpaper in preparation for painting.

CUT OUT BIRD SHAPE

6. Use a photocopier to enlarge the red bird pattern (below) 200% and cut out the bird shape.

7. Trace bird onto lauan; cut out with the jigsaw.

8. Using a hole saw attached to a screw gun or drill, bore a 1¼-in. to 1½-in. hole in the lauan. This is the bird's entrance, so be sure to place it accordingly.

9. Sand the face and edges smooth in preparation for painting.

PAINT AND ASSEMBLE

10. Prime and paint the outside of the box and bird shape, leaving the inside unpainted.

11. Hinge the bird cutout to the box using a simple 1-in. butt hinge or similar connector (see Photo 1).

12. Attach 1 screw eye with hook to the back of the bird and other screw eye to the side of the box so they meet when the hook closes (see Photo 2).

13. Seal the outside of birdhouse with several coats of shellac.

14. Attach picture-hanging hardware to the back of the box.

PHOTO 1

PHOTO 2

BIRD PATTERN

Use a photocopier to enlarge the red bird pattern 200%.

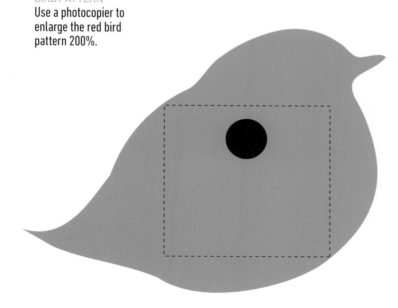

BREAK THE MOLD

You don't have to pay a lot for a one-of-a-kind birdbath. This year, look for plants with large leaves to add to your garden. Then turn one of those big beauties into a lovely custom birdbath. It makes a serene resting place for butterflies as well.

MATERIALS

- **Large leaf**
- **½ to 1 bag of play sand**
- **3 to 4 cups of contractor's sand**
- **1 to 2 cups Portland cement**
- **Concrete fortifier**

DIRECTIONS

1. Choose a leaf at least 10 in. long and 7 in. wide. (We used a hosta leaf here, but rhubarb, burdock, gunnera, castor bean, caladium and elephant-ear leaves also work well.) Cut the stem off.

2. Spread out a sheet of plastic or a large plastic bag to protect your work surface. Pour the play sand onto the plastic and make a pile. Wet the sand slightly so that it sticks together, the way you would for a sand castle.

3. Shape the pile to approximate the size and shape of your leaf, but keep in mind that birds do not like baths that are more than a couple of inches deep. Once the sand pile is to your liking, cover it with a piece of plastic or a plastic bag. Place the leaf, vein side up, on top of the plastic, centering it.

4. In a plastic bowl, mix 3 parts contractor's sand to 1 part Portland cement. Mix ¼ cup of water and ¼ cup of concrete fortifier, and add slowly to the sand until it reaches the consistency of a thick brownie batter. The easiest way to do this is to squish it with your hands, wearing rubber gloves. Mix more water and fortifier to add to the sand if needed. Rinse your gloves or hands. Pick up a handful of the sand mixture, plop it on the center of the leaf and spread to the edges. This gives you a solid surface that picks up the leaf's veining while removing air bubbles.

5. Now slowly start building up the thickness of the casting. For strength, keep it between ½ and 1 in. thick. Be careful to keep the edges smooth to get a good contour. Once you have the casting at a good thickness, build up the center to make a pedestal.

6. Cover the mixture loosely with plastic. If it's a hot day, you might want to mist the casting from time to time to keep it from drying out too fast and cracking. Let your project dry slowly for about 24 hours, then peel off the leaf. If casting feels brittle, let it sit for another day.

7. After the casting has dried for a good week, you can paint or seal it. (We painted it green.) Or simply leave it as is and enjoy!

HANDMADE HELPER

You can leave your birdbath out year-round, but if it's painted or stained, you might want to bring it inside during winter. Clean it just as you would any other birdbath, using a sponge or small brush once a week.

CRAFT: DOTTIE BALTZ

SUPPLIES

STEP 3

STEP 5

STEP 6

SODA BOTTLE BIRD FEEDER

Create a feeding station that positively pops for the seed eaters that like to visit your backyard.

MATERIALS

- **Glass soda bottle with cap**
- **¼-in. threaded steel rod, 12 in. long**
- **7¼x7½-in. turnbuckle with 2 eye bolts**
- **Loctite glue**
- **Chicken feeder**
- **Washer**
- **¼-in. threaded wing nut**
- **G-hook**
- **1-in. diamond drill bit**
- **½-in. regular twist drill bit**

DIRECTIONS

1. Glass soda bottles aren't hard to find these days. Mexican Coca-Cola is usually sold this way, and it's readily available across the United States. Once you have the bottle (this example uses a 1-liter bottle), find something to hold the neck to keep it in place. The garbage disposal opening in your kitchen sink may be ideal for this.

2. Next, under running water, use a 1-in. diamond drill bit to make a hole in the bottom of the bottle. This is the most difficult part of the project. It's important to keep your drill bit and glass cool by immersing them in water; overheating can break the bottle and even ruin your bit. Start at an angle, gently holding the drill bit in place. Once the drill bit has made a groove in the glass, straighten the bit up so that it hits all sides of the hole evenly. Run your drill at a slow speed to start out, speeding up as the bit becomes deeper, then slowing down toward the end. Once you've made the hole, you may need to file the sharp edges; an emery board will do.

3. With the ½-in. drill bit, drill a hole in the center of the chicken feeder and the Coke bottle cap.

4. Connect the turnbuckle and the steel rod by removing one of the eye hooks from the turnbuckle and screwing the rod into place. Once you've determined that you have the correct length, you can use a drop or two of Loctite to keep it from moving, but don't do this until you have put it together successfully at least once.

5. Taking out the other eye hook, place it through the drilled hole in the bottle cap and screw it back into the turnbuckle. The eye of the eye bolt will be on top of the cap for your hanging hook to thread through.

6. Feed the steel rod through the top of the bottle, past the hole in the bottom of the bottle and then through the hole in the chicken feeder. Firmly press the bottle cap down on the lip of the bottle.

7. Holding the feeder upside down, place the washer over the threaded rod. Last, screw the wing nut in place.

8. Attach a hook. We used a G-hook, but you may choose a different type depending on where you want to hang it.

9. Once you're ready to fill your bird feeder, simply take the bottom off, fill the feeder with your favorite seed and reattach the bottom.

10. Finally, find the best place in your yard to hang your creation so that you and the birds can enjoy it!

• • •

TIN CAN FLOWER FEEDERS

What could be more cheery and charming than these tiny feeders? They bring a cottagey feel to the backyard.

MATERIALS

○ Clean, opened tin cans with labels removed
○ Spray paint in choice of colors
○ Precut 6-in.-wide foam flowers (available at most craft stores)
○ Large wooden or plastic beads
○ Hot glue gun and glue sticks
○ Thick twine
○ Drill with drill bits or metal punch

DIRECTIONS

1. On the side of each tin can, use a ruler to measure about ¼ in. from each end in a straight line. Mark a dot at each of these points with a permanent marker. Use a drill or metal punch to make holes about ¼ in. wide where the marked dots are. (These holes are where you will insert the twine for making a hanger later on.)

2. In a well-ventilated area, spray-paint the outside of your tin cans in various colors. Apply as many coats as needed for full coverage and let dry 24-48 hours.

3. Lay the open end of each can centered on a foam flower. Trace around the circle opening with a pencil. Working either freehand or using a compass, draw another circle about ½ in. smaller inside the circle. Then use a ruler to draw several crisscrossing straight lines inside the original traced circle (similar to slices of a round pizza). First cut out the small inner circle. Cut along each crisscrossing line, stopping at the traced outline of the original circle. This will make several tabs around the inner edge.

4. Lay the foam flower face down on a flat surface. Apply a ring of hot glue around the perimeter of the traced circle. Then place the open end of the can aligned on top of the hot glue ring. Hold the can firmly in place until the glue dries. Hot-glue each of the cut tabs down on the interior of the can rim to further secure the foam flower in place.

5. For the hangers, first cut a 12- to 18-in. piece of twine for each can. Thread 1 end through the back hole, inside the can and back up through the front hole. With even lengths of twine, place several large beads on each loose end. Knot the top of the twine to secure the hanger with beads in place. Repeat to find second tin can feeder.

ORANGE WREATH FOR ORIOLES

Orioles love fresh oranges and are also attracted to the color orange, so these wreaths are the perfect enticement. Hang one near a sturdy branch so an oriole has a perch from which to peck!

MATERIALS

○ Wire coat hanger with a cardboard tube
○ Needle-nose pliers (or strong hands)
○ Wire cutters
○ Oranges
○ Cutting board
○ Good slicing kitchen knife
○ Ribbon and berries (optional)

DIRECTIONS

1. Remove the cardboard tube from hanger and bend the 2 sides of the hanger toward each other until they are spaced about 1 in. apart.

2. Form the wire into a rustic bird shape, as shown. Using your hands may be the easiest way to start. Then use needle-nose pliers to refine the shape and smooth any rough curves.

3. Use pliers or a wire cutter to snip the curled ends off the hanger.

4. Cut oranges into about ¼-in. slices. Cut little pieces of rind from the orange ends into roughly ½-in. triangles. These will serve as spacers between the slices and help keep everything in place.

5. Thread an orange slice through both wires. Then thread a piece of rind next to it on one or both wires.

6. Repeat step 5, threading more oranges, until you run out of wire.

7. Tie a little bow around the bird's neck and add some berries at the end if you wish. Hang from a tree close to a window so you can see the orioles when they come for a snack!

ORANGE WREATH: CRAFT, ALISON AUTH; PHOTO, HEIDI HESS

SILVERWARE SUET FEEDER

Your backyard birds deserve a fine dining experience, so serve up their suet in this elegant yet functional holder for a suet cake. Old silverware holds the suet in place for a whimsical way to feed birds. It takes only a little while to put together—and before you know it, backyard birds will be lining up for a seat at the table.

MATERIALS

- **Weathered board, 2 ft. long and at least 9 in. wide**
- **Silver-plated flatware, 5 pieces**
- **Hinge**
- **Wire, 18 in. long, 20-gauge**
- **Screws, assorted sizes to fit hinge holes and drilled silverware**
- **Drill bits**
- **Scrap piece of 2-by-4**
- **Drill press or hand drill**
- **Nail**
- **Rubber mallet**
- **Screwdriver**
- **Wire cutter**
- **Pliers**
- **Safety goggles**
- **Gloves**
- **Wrapped suet cake**

DIRECTIONS

1. Pound silverware as flat as you can with a rubber mallet. The more rustic it looks, the better!

2. Use the nail to make divots in handles of the silverware to keep the drill bit from skipping.

3. With safety goggles on, drill holes with drill press or hand drill, keeping drill bit perpendicular to silverware.

4. To make the first bend, place 1 piece of silverware, decorative side up, on a sturdy surface. Place 2-by-4 on top of the handle, and bend the silverware up at a 90-degree angle. Wear gloves if you'd like, and repeat with remaining silverware.

5. To determine where silverware should go, place a wrapped suet cake on the weathered board; mark with a pencil. Place silverware on the board to hold suet, and attach with screws.

6. Make the second bend by placing the 2-by-4 flush with each piece of silverware and bending the silverware over the 2-by-4. Refer to photo. Use the rubber mallet to help, if necessary.

7. Attach a hinge to the back of the board. The tubular part of the hinge should be just above the edge.

8. String wire through the center of the hinge and curl it with pliers to make decorative loops for hanging.

9. Remove the wrapper from a store-bought suet cake, but leave it in the plastic tray. Insert into the feeder.

NOTE: This feeder was designed to hold a store-bought suet cake that is still in its plastic tray. If you'd like to try using homemade suet, place it in a plastic tray first to help it keep its shape.

CRAFT: LINDA HILDERBRAND, THE SALVAGE STUDIO

• • •

IT'S TEATIME

Repurpose a mismatched or slightly damaged teacup and saucer by turning it into a lovely bird feeder.

MATERIALS

- Cup and saucer
- Spoon or fork
- 14- and 19-gauge galvanized wire
- Drill
- Tile drill bit
- Nut and bolt (depends on the size of drill bit you are using)
- Needle-nose pliers
- Beads (about ten 6-10 mm beads and 4 more beads with a larger hole)
- Hammer
- Safety goggles

DIRECTIONS

1. Drill a hole on the side of the teacup opposite the handle. Use the tile drill bit, but drill slowly and apply minimal pressure to avoid cracking the cup. Next, drill a hole in the center of the cup bottom and center of the saucer.

2. Cut 2 pieces, about 10 in. each, of 19-gauge wire. Fold each piece of wire in half to make a small loop. Hold the loop with the pliers and twist about 5 times to make a hook at the top. Leave about 4 in. of wire on each side.

3. Insert 1 of the wire ends into the hole in the cup from the inside out. Make the loop tight so that it rests on the rim. Twist the ends together to close the loop. Coil the excess with the pliers.

4. With the second piece of wire, make another small loop, which will sit on top of the cup's handle. Try to make the loop about the same height as the other one. Depending on the placement of the handle, you might need to make more twists. Once they're close to the same height, wrap the excess wire around the handle.

5. Take 16 in. of 14-gauge wire and fold it in half to make a "V" shape about 4 in. high. Using the pliers, coil the ends into decorative swirls.

6. Press the piece by laying the wire on an anvil or hard surface and flatten with a hammer. This will prevent the wire from uncoiling.

7. Add beads to the V shape by wrapping 19-gauge wire around it, adding a bead every 3 to 5 wraps.

8. For the attachment pieces, use 3 pieces of 19-gauge wire and 2 beads. Thread 1 bead and bend 2 eye hooks on each end. Repeat for the other 2 wires.

9. Attach 1 end of each attachment piece to the swirls of the V shape. Attach the other ends to hooks at the top of the cup.

10. Attach the saucer to the cup using the nut and bolt. Gently tighten, being careful not to crack the cup or saucer.

11. Flatten the bowl of the spoon using a hammer. To roll the spoon to use it as a hook, gently tap the tip of the bowl. It will start folding or rolling, depending on the material the spoon is made of.

12. Cut a 38-in. length of 14-gauge wire and make a swirl at 1 end. Press the swirl with a hammer so it doesn't uncurl.

13. Insert the opposite end of the wire into the fold of the spoon. Wrap the wire around the spoon a few times and add beads.

14. When you get to the top of the spoon, there should be about 4 to 8 in. of wire left. At the end, make a hook with the pliers. Start by making a small loop, and then make a "U" at the end. Press this hook.

15. Connect the spoon hanger to the rest of the feeder using the attachment bead. Now you're ready to add some birdseed.

WINE CORK BIRDHOUSE

This might be one of the simplest—yet most impressive—DIY projects you'll ever find because all you really need to know how to do is glue. Just grab a premade birdhouse and let the crafting fun begin!

MATERIALS
- **Birdhouse**
- **About 50-60 corks**
- **Band saw or serrated knife**
- **Outdoor-grade glue**
- **Dremel tool**

DIRECTIONS
1. Buy or build a birdhouse. One with a 1⅛-in. entrance hole is standard for most songbirds. A house with an overhang is nice because it protects the entrance from the elements.
2. Cut the corks in half lengthwise with a table band saw or a sharp serrated knife, which will give you a nice, flat gluing surface. If you want to skip cutting the corks, you can use whole ones. You'll just need more corks and a little more glue per piece.
3. Glue the corks on in any pattern you like, trimming with a serrated knife as needed. Either wood or silicone glue will work.
4. Use a Dremel tool to round the corks around the entrance hole. If you don't have a Dremel, a serrated knife will work.
5. For the roof, glue the cork halves directly on top. If you're patient, slice the corks into disks to create a pretty shingled effect.

> **HANDMADE HELPER**
> You don't have to buy new. Refurbish an old birdhouse with this project, too.

5-MINUTE FEEDER

You don't have to do a lot of work to attract orioles. The bright orange fliers will gladly flock to this feeder filled with grape jelly or sugar water. It's a simple project that is perfect for gauging oriole interest in your area. You can do it in less than five minutes, and it'll cost only a couple of bucks at most.

MATERIALS
- **3 ft. 10-gauge copper wire**
- **12 in. 18-gauge copper wire**
- **Double shot glass (3 oz.)**
- **Wire strippers or cutters**
- **Needle-nose pliers**
- **Pen**
- **Glass beads**

DIRECTIONS
1. Using the needle-nose pliers, make a small hook at one end of the 10-gauge wire. This will be the feeder's hanger.
2. Starting at the hanger end, gently bend the wire into an arch. You can use a round object to help with this, or you can bend it freehand.
3. Approximately 12 in. from the hanger end, bend the wire at about a 45-degree angle. Place the shot glass on top of the wire and bend the wire around bottom of glass.
4. Cup the wire and glass in your hand while wrapping most of the remaining wire tightly around the glass.
5. At this point, you should have about 6 to 8 in. of wire remaining. Curve it into a "C" shape in front of the glass to make a perch.
6. To help the feeder hang better, gently twist the hanger portion a quarter turn to the right or left.
7. To decorate, wrap the 18-gauge copper wire around the 10-gauge wire near the top of the hanger. Wrap the last few inches of wire around a pen to form a curlicue.
8. Add beads in alternating sizes. To secure the beads, curl the end of the wire with needle-nose pliers.

• • •

BLUEBIRD BED-AND-BREAKFAST

This whimsical design offers a colorful alternative to ordinary bluebird houses. To make it yourself, just buy or build a plain bluebird nest box and dress it up to make an attractive B&B.

MATERIALS

- **Bluebird house (or wood or recycled material to make your own)**
- **Plant holder with dish to fit**
- **Base of your choice**
- **Roofing material of your choice**
- **Material for clean-out door, including hinge, handle, etc.**
- **Paint**
- **Clear shellac sealer**
- **Assorted screws or nails**
- **Cordless drill**
- **Jigsaw or coping saw**
- **Snips**
- **Drill bits**

DIRECTIONS

1. If making your own birdhouse, old columns cut to size make it easy. All you need to do is add a roof, a bottom, a door and whatever adornments tickle your fancy. An architectural salvage yard is a great place to find columns, skeleton keys, old door hardware and cabinet knobs, hooks of all shapes and sizes, orphaned light canopies and other assorted castaways. If you don't have a column lying around, don't fret. Four pieces of wood cut to size and nailed together will put you in business.

2. Use any kind of flexible, water-impervious material to make the roof. Rubber, Sunbrella fabric scraps, tin, copper and aluminum flashing are all possibilities. (The roof of this house uses tin flashing.) If you have something that will work but you don't like the look of it, paint it with glue and press sheet moss over it. This provides a gorgeous green roof, and the birds love pulling out bits of moss for their nests!

3. Cut out the entrance hole and door before putting the bottom on the house, using a jigsaw or old-fashioned coping saw. Hinge the door with a little strip of rubber or fabric, or a small metal hinge.

4. Perches right in front of the entrance hole can pose a real threat to baby birds and eggs. Squirrels and other predators use them to extend their reach into the house. It's much better to have perches on the side of the house. In this example, we attached a wrought-iron plant holder that can double as a side perch, as well as a convenient place to leave food or fresh water.

5. A predator guard can be anything applied to the entrance hole to add depth. You can use radiator and plumbing supply escutcheons, porcelain light sockets, or even a block of wood with the same size hole drilled in it and nailed over the existing hole. Anything that makes it harder for a squirrel or raccoon paw to reach inside the house will do!

6. Paint and adornments of all kinds can make your house one of a kind. (Whether you paint or not, remember to use a top coat of clear shellac sealer for weather protection.) The wrought-iron plant holder on the side of this house presents several options. You can use it for a live plant, or turn it into a year-round feeder for bluebirds and fill it with mealworms. Use your imagination, and you will have a B&B no bluebird could resist!

HOUSE BASICS

Whether you buy a basic bluebird house or decide to make your own, there are a few necessities. First, make sure it has ventilation holes at the top, drainage holes in the bottom and a clean-out door for annual maintenance.

The house should have a 5x5-in. floor, a height of 8 to 12 in. and an entrance hole of 1½ in. placed 6 to 10 in. above the floor. Mount the house 4 to 5 feet above the ground toward an open field on a fence, post, utility pole or tree.

EASY-TO-MAKE FEEDERS

This feeder is inexpensive and simple to create. It makes a great project for the kids on a rainy day. Grab a few supplies and get crafting!

MATERIALS

- Bucket
- Water
- Newspaper (about 10 pages, cut in strips)
- Duct tape
- Window screen
- Drill with drill bits
- Fishing line
- Beads
- Peanut butter
- Birdseed
- Wire hanger

DIRECTIONS

1. Fill a bucket half full with water and add newspaper strips. Allow the paper to soak for about 15 minutes. Then squish and roll the paper in your hands to extract the water. Repeat this process a few times until the paper is in very small pieces.
2. Use duct tape to attach a window screen to the top of the bucket.
3. Rinse the pieces of paper a few more times by pouring them over the screen to remove most of the water. Squish and roll the paper again; put in a clean bucket of water. Repeat until most of the ink is washed away.
4. Pour the paper over your screen one last time. Allow it to sit for a while so most of the water is removed. You want it wet, but not so wet it won't mold into a shape. Begin shaping the paper into a softball-sized heart (or a shape of your choice).

The base of your paper feeder should be about an inch thick. Allow it to dry.
5. Drill a hole through the top of each side of the heart. Thread a piece of fishing line through 1 hole, tie and add beads. Thread the line through the other hole and tie.
6. Spread peanut butter on each side of the paper heart feeder and dip into birdseed. Then just hang it up!

FEEDER FROM A FRAME

If you have an unused picture frame lying around—maybe the glass broke, or you found it at a thrift store—turn it into a delightful bird feeder.

MATERIALS

- Old picture frame
- 4 screw eyes
- Chain or wire for hanging
- Shower curtain hanger or something similar for gathering the chain
- Window screen
- Paint
- Staple gun and staples
- Wire cutters (if using stiff chain)
- Snips or scissors for cutting screen
- Hammer and finish nail or drill for pilot holes

DIRECTIONS

1. Paint picture frame, if desired.
2. Cut screen to fit the picture frame opening and staple it to back of frame. (If staples are poking through the front of the frame, caulk over them as we did to create a mock filigree.)
3. Using either a hammer and finish nail or drill bit, make pilot holes in the four corners of the finished side of the frame for the screw eyes. Twist in the screw eyes.
4. Cut four equal lengths of chain or wire and attach one to each screw eye. Gather at the top and run the shower curtain hanger through the ends of the chain. Hang from a branch.

CRAFT: ALISON AUTH; PHOTO: HEIDI HESS

BURNING BEAUTY

Build your own birdhouse from scratch and add an elegant personal touch with a burned-in pattern.

MATERIALS

- **One 5-ft. 1-by-6 No. 2 common pine board**
- **Handsaw or compound miter saw**
- **Power drill and bits**
- **1¼- to 1⅝-in. spade bit or hole saw**
- **Eight 1⅝-in. galvanized deck screws**
- **Six 2-in. galvanized finishing nails**
- **Fine-grit sandpaper**
- **Carbon or tracing paper (optional)**
- **Wood-burning kit or pen**
- **Sponge or honing paper**

DIRECTIONS

1. Measure and cut the pine board into 5 pieces:
A. 10-in. piece for front
B. 10-in. piece for roof
C. 7¾-in. piece for back
D. 18-in. piece for sides
E. 4-in. piece for floor
Save the remaining scrap board for wood-burning practice.
2. For sides, on D, measure and mark a spot 8 in. from the left along top edge, and 10 in. from the left along the bottom. Draw a diagonal line connecting these points. Cut along this line to yield 2 side walls, each with an 8-in. and a 10-in. side.

3. With spade bit or hole saw, on A (front), drill entrance hole 2-2½ in. from a short side.
4. On front side of A, drill through each corner with a narrow bit, then attach A to 10-in. sides of D with four 1⅝-in. deck screws.
5. Attach C (back) to center of the 8-in. sides of D with two 2-in. finishing nails. Predrill holes in C (back) using a slightly smaller bit.
6. Cut about ½ in. off each corner of E (floor) for drainage gaps when house is complete.
7. Set the floor ¼ in. up from the bottom of the house, then attach it with four 2-in. finishing nails at the sides and back. (Do not nail the floor at the front, or you won't be able to unscrew the birdhouse front for cleaning.)
8. Attach B (roof) to top at sides with four 1⅝-in. deck screws. Predrill holes in B with a narrow bit.

BURNING

9. Sand exterior of the birdhouse until smooth, including the entrance hole, with fine-grit sandpaper.
10. Use carbon paper to trace a design onto the wood, or draw it freehand.
11. With the burner pen at the desired temperature, follow the pattern, being careful not to put too much pressure on the pen tip. When the pattern is finished, hang the birdhouse in your favorite backyard spot.

WOOD-BURNING TIPS

- Before you start burning the pattern onto the birdhouse, practice on a scrap of pine to determine the best heat setting and to get comfortable with the process.
- Because of the heat, carbon will build up on the metal pen tips. Keep a damp sponge or honing paper near the work space to wipe off the tip.
- For the cleanest lines, go slowly and maintain consistent pressure. You can change the look of the burn by altering the pressure and the length of time the tip is on the wood.

BOTTLE-FEEDING HUMMINGBIRDS

Treat these favorite fliers to a sleek, shiny, custom-decorated sugar-water dispenser. You'll be amazed at how fun and easy it is to make this one-of-a-kind hummingbird feeder using a recycled glass bottle. For a few dollars and a small time investment, you'll have a pretty copper-accented addition to your backyard.

MATERIALS

- **Glass bottle, 12 oz. or smaller**
- **5 ft. of 4-gauge untreated copper wire**
- **3 to 5 ft. of 12-gauge untreated copper wire**
- **Hummingbird feeding tube**
- **Beads or other decorations**
- **D ring or carabiner**
- **Screw eye**
- **File**
- **Needle-nose pliers**
- **Wire cutter**

DIRECTIONS

1. File the ends of the copper wires so there are no sharp edges.
2. Take the 4-gauge wire and bend it at 1 end to form a small circle that fits loosely over the opening of the bottle.
3. Insert the bottle and make another loop around the neck to hold it securely.
4. With the neck of the bottle securely in the 2 loops, wind the rest of the wire around the bottle. (This is where you have a little freedom to make your own design.) The wire should be loose enough to remove the bottle for refilling the sugar water, but tight enough to hold the feeder securely.
5. Bend the last 18 in. or so of 4-gauge wire upward to make a hanging hook and then fashion a loop at the very end to secure it.
6. Decorate feeder using the 12-gauge copper wire. Use needle-nose pliers and wire cutters to shape the wire as needed. To create a curling-vine effect, wrap wire around a pencil and then attach it in pieces.
7. Use some colorful beads or other adornments to complete your design. Remember, hummingbirds love red, so it's a great accent color.

8. Remove the bottle and fill it with sugar water. Then take your store-bought feeding tube and gently twist the stopper into place at the opening of the bottle. It should fit snugly to avoid leaking.
9. Put the bottle back in the copper holder. You might have to shake the bottle a little to dislodge any air bubbles. If it leaks, remove the feeding tube and try repositioning the stopper to get a tighter fit.
10. Ready to put your feeder to work? Make sure it hangs securely by hooking the feeder onto a snap ring or carabiner. Then put the ring through a screw eye and hang the feeder wherever you like.

STEP 5

STEP 6

STEP 9

> **HANDMADE HELPER**
> Use a bottle that is no larger than 12 oz. (about 375 ml) and will provide a tight fit for the stopper portion of the feeding tube you buy. Anything less than an airtight fit will allow the nectar to drip from the feeding tube. Many soda bottles are a good fit for a commercial tube-feeder assembly. Be sure to test the seal before you complete your design and add sugar water.

CRAFT: BILL MERRITT

Fuss-Free and FUNCTIONAL

CLASSIC PLANT MARKERS

Finding plant markers that can withstand sun, wind and rain is a challenge. And you want them to be attractive, easy to make and reusable year after year. These attractive, durable plant markers are the perfect solution. Don't limit yourself to the shapes shown here. Be creative! With some copper sheet metal and wire, you can make a bushelful in no time. The best part...they're sure to last. Unless you run them over with the lawn mower!

MATERIALS

- 36-gauge copper sheets
- 12-gauge wire
- Paint marker, extra fine, black
- Colored paint marker (optional)
- Transparent tape
- Clear enamel spray
- Scissors
- Paper punch (optional)
- Side cutting pliers
- Small rubber or plastic roller (optional)
- Soldering gun or mini torch (larger torches are not recommended for this small project)
- Solder and flux
- Incombustible soldering surface
- Fine sandpaper, 220-grit
- Fine steel wool

DIRECTIONS

1. Make your own paper patterns and cut them out, leaving about ⅛ in. border around edges. Tape patterns to copper sheet metal. Cut the copper along the outline of each shape using scissors. Sand sharp edges. Punch any holes desired with a paper punch. Flatten each shape with a roller, rolling pin or a glass bottle on a smooth surface.

2. Place the copper shapes on a soft pad (such as a dish towel) and write plant names with a blunt pencil. Use a black paint marker to write within the indents, making the names more prominent. Decorate the edges if desired.

3. Clean shapes and wires with steel wool or sandpaper before soldering.

4. Cut wire with side cutting pliers to desired length (ours are about 10 in.). Solder wire to the back of each marker. Apply flux first and heat until it bubbles. Then touch the solder to the side of the wire until it flows. Solder on both sides of the wire, holding the wire in place until it cools. Spray the markers with clear enamel to prevent tarnishing.

> **HANDMADE HELPER**
> When working with a soldering gun or torch, keep a fire extinguisher or a bucket of water close by. It's better to have it nearby and not need it. Remember that the metal stays hot for a while after it's been heated. Handle finished pieces with pliers until they cool.

CRAFT: PAT KERR

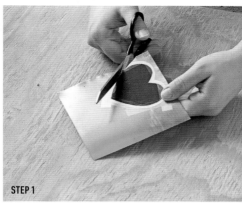

STEP 1

STEP 2

STEP 3

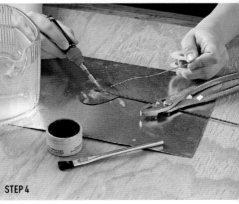

STEP 4

REMOTE GARDEN CUBBY

Keep tools and supplies right next to your garden with this small storage house. It only takes a few hours to build, and can be made with pine or rough-sawn cedar as shown here.

MATERIALS LIST

QTY.	SIZE & DESCRIPTION
2	8-ft. 1x12 cedar or pine boards
1	8-ft. 4x4 post
1 set	2x2-in. mortise hinges
1	magnetic catch
1 lb.	1½-in. galvanized finish nails

CUTTING LIST

KEY	QTY.	SIZE & DESCRIPTION
A	1	11x15¾-in. door
B	2	9½x15⅞-in. sides
C	1	11¼x8-in. bottom
D	1	11¼x15⅞-in. back
E	2	12¾x6½-in. gables
F	1	11¼x12¾-in. long roof panel
G	1	11¼x12-in. short roof panel
H	2	11¼x2½-in. rafters

NOTE: All dimensions are for ¾-in.-thick wood.

DIRECTIONS

1. Cut flat, dry 1x12s to the sizes in the Cutting List. Nail and glue the sides, base and back together, then attach the rafters and gables.

2. Fasten shorter roof panel on 1 side, leaving ⅞-in. overhangs in the front and back. Caulk the top edge, then nail on the long panel.

3. Cut the hinge mortises into the door and side, and hang the door. Stain or paint the wood inside and out to seal it. Use branches for the handle, nailing them in place.

FIGURE A
EXPLODED VIEW

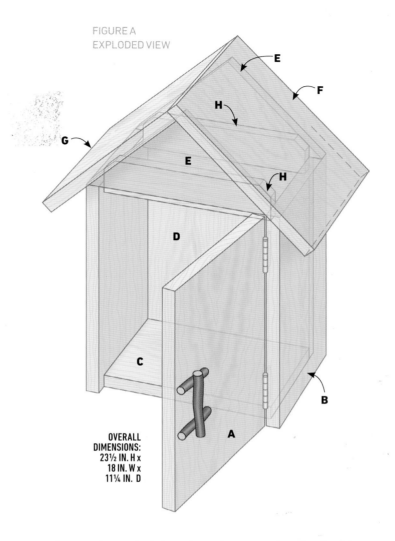

OVERALL DIMENSIONS:
23½ IN. H x
18 IN. W x
11¼ IN. D

RUSTIC DOOR HANDLE

To make a door handle from a tree branch, nail the crosspieces to the door with brad nails. Then notch the back of the handle so it sits flat on the crosspieces and nail it into place.

STICK 'EM UP

Household notes will stay put on a washboard memo station that also doubles as a handy cupboard.

MATERIALS

- **Washboard with metal corrugated section**
- **¾-in. wood, 3½ in. wide and 8½ ft. long**
- **Particleboard**
- **2 hinges**
- **Small cabinet doorknob**
- **Soda caps**
- **Vintage spice tins**
- **Adhesive magnets**
- **Nails and screws**
- **Drill**
- **Nail gun or hammer**
- **Wood stain, optional**
- **Foam brushes or rag, optional**

DIRECTIONS

1. Measure washboard from bottom of legs to about 1 in. from the top. Cut 2 pieces of the ¾-in. wood to that length for the sides of the cupboard.
2. Measure the width of the washboard. Cut 2 pieces of ¾-in. wood to that length minus 1½ in. for the top and bottom of the cupboard.
3. Nail 2 sides, top and bottom together to create a box frame.
4. Cut the desired number of shelves from the remaining ¾-in. wood, using the length of the top and bottom pieces as a guide. Nail the shelf pieces into place in the box.
5. Measure height and width of the box frame and cut a piece of particleboard to fit. Nail the particleboard to the back of the box frame.
6. Stain the box to match the washboard finish, if desired.
7. Place washboard on top of the box and determine where the hinges best fit. Drill pilot holes and screw the hinges in place on the box and the washboard.
8. Screw the doorknob onto the leg of the washboard opposite the hinges.
9. Hang cupboard on the wall and place magnets on the metal washboard. Fill spice tins with pencils and pens.

STUCK TIGHT

To make these magnets, empty spice tins and remove lids; remove the caps from glass soda bottles. Wash and dry thoroughly. Cut adhesive magnet strips to fit the backs of the tins and soda caps. Apply magnets to tins and caps.

HAMMOCK BLANKET

Put old denim jeans to work again as a pretty and practical new piece.

MATERIALS

- **10-15 pairs old jeans**
- **Hammock**
- **2-4 spools heavy-duty blue thread**
- **2 yd. of 1-in. strapping**
- **6 parachute buckles**
- **Sewing machine**

DIRECTIONS

1. Cut the skinniest pair of jeans along 1 inseam. Measure denim width to determine maximum size of each square, which will require a ½-in. seam allowance all around.

2. Measure hammock area. Calculate number of squares needed to cover hammock bed, allowing for a few extra inches to hang over each long side. Cut squares to size out of jeans and arrange in preferred pattern.

3. Placing the wrong sides together, sew squares to each other in a column with a ½-in. seam. Sew columns to each other with a ½-in. seam, with wrong sides together. Sew a ½-in. border around perimeter. Fringe squares by making ¼-in. cuts about ¼ in. apart along each seam. Wash cover to fray the fringe. Dry blanket thoroughly.

4. Lay blanket over hammock and mark 3 places on each end where a strap can wrap around crossbar.

5. Cut strapping into six 12-in. pieces. Thread 1 piece through 1 end of a buckle, fold over, and stitch securely. Repeat with the other end of strap and the other side of buckle. Stitch strapping securely to back of blanket where it was marked in Step 4. Repeat for all 6 straps.

6. Attach blanket to hammock.

CRAFTS: CUPBOARD, STEPHANIE SLIWINSKI; HAMMOCK BLANKET, SAMANTHA BENDER

UPCYCLED BIRD FEEDER

Turn old odds and ends into a unique bird feeder with this eye-fetching craft.

MATERIALS

- **Threaded rod**
- **A section of pipe or the bottom portion of a floor lamp (for the base)**
- **Hubcap, the older the better**
- **Kitchen steamer**
- **Lamp parts**
- **Coffee percolator parts**
- **Garden hose connections**
- **Dangles**
- **Connectors for dangles**
- **Metal punch or hammer and nail**

INSTRUCTIONS

1. To begin, look for items to stack that may already have holes or openings in the center.

2. Most likely you will need to punch or drill a hole in the center of your hubcap, just big enough for your threaded rod to slip through. Punch holes through it, and any of the other pieces that need a center opening, with a heavy-duty metal punch or a hammer and nail.

3. Experiment with stacking your metal pieces. Just start on a flat surface and layer away. It's fun to have a piece to hang things from under your hubcap; try a vegetable steamer facing downward for a playful look.

4. When you like your combination, take one of the metal nuts and thread it on the rod about 12 in. below the top. Slide on your bottom piece and add another nut for a secure base.

5. Next, add your hubcap and the other pieces. The best part of this project is that you can change your mind as often as you want!

6. To finish off your stack, slip on the third metal nut and tighten until your pieces stay securely side by side. You might have to adjust the bottom nuts to go higher or lower along the rod.

7. If you don't want the nut on top showing, glue on a finial, such as a hose connector. Use sturdy, waterproof glue. One of our favorites, the Marine formula made by Amazing Goop, is UV resistant and easy to apply.

8. Now it's time to embellish your feeder with dangles. Suspend camping cups, crystal chandelier drops, beads, bobbins, mystery parts or whatever you fancy from the built-in openings or from holes you punch around the edges of one or more layers. Easy connectors are large paper clips, split rings or binder rings. At first your feathered friends might be timid of the accessories, but give them some time to get used to it.

9. Your threaded rod will slip inside a section of pipe, which can then be inserted into a garden pot or a planting bed. If you want a free-standing piece, you can slip the rod inside the base and pole of a socket-free, semi-disassembled floor lamp.

10. Add birdseed and enjoy.

CRAFTS: BETH EVANS-RAMOS, THE SALVAGE STUDIO

PUP PRIMPING STATION

Give a vintage washtub new life when you create this washing station for your pooch.

MATERIALS

- Galvanized washtub
- Distressed wood
- Circular saw
- Drill with a metal drill bit
- Screws
- Hook

DIRECTIONS

1. Measure the interior width of the washtub where the shelf will be placed. Cut the piece of wood to that length.
2. Drill 2 holes on each side of the washtub at the point where the shelf will sit. Align the shelf inside. Drive screws through the washtub into the wood, securing it in place.
3. Drill a hole in the bottom of the washtub to align with the hook. Screw the hook into place.
4. Drill 2 holes in the bottom of the washtub. Hang the tub near an exterior faucet using screws driven through the holes. Drape a hose around the outside and attach to the faucet.

CANDLES IN THE SAND

Pretty up a picnic with an easy-to-make sand candle. Ours suits a star-spangled get-together, but you can create any simple shape you'd like.

MATERIALS

- 1-lb. bag of soy wax flakes
- All-purpose or play sand
- Waxed 3½-in. wire wick with clip
- Candle wax dye

DIRECTIONS

1. Dampen sand 4-5 in. deep in a bucket, a sturdy cardboard box or a sandbox. Dig out a star shape 7-8 in. across and 2-3 in. deep. Make a small, shallow circle in the center to help the finished candle sit flat on a table.
2. Melt wax flakes and dye in a double boiler over medium heat. Slowly pour melted wax into sand while holding wick in the center of the star. Allow wax to harden completely, about 4 hours. Trim wick to about 1 in.
3. Dig carefully around the candle until you can lift it out. Lightly brush off any excess sand.

MAGNIFICENT BIRDBATH LAMP

Turn an old lamp into a water park for your feathered friends.

MATERIALS

○ **Old lamp**
○ **Painter's tape**
○ **Spray primer and paint**
○ **Wide, shallow bowl for bath**
○ **Clear epoxy**
○ **Ceiling light canopy** (optional)

DIRECTIONS

1. Remove the socket and lampshade support from the lamp and cut the cord at both ends to make it easy to pull through the lamp housing.

2. You can add a ceiling light canopy to the top of the lamp to offer more support to the bowl. This is simple to do, since a ceiling light canopy already has a hole in the center, and the lamp has a screw and nut, making attachment super easy. (You may need to add a washer if the nut on the lamp is smaller than the canopy hole.)

3. It's much easier to paint the lamp before adding the bowl. Make sure to wash the lamp for a dust-free surface, and let dry thoroughly. We used painter's tape to protect the base of the lamp.

4. Several light coats of spray paint within a few minutes of each other provide a quick transformation.

5. When the paint is thoroughly dry, usually within an hour or two, you can glue the bowl onto the circular canopy edge. We used a clear epoxy out of the tube all around the bowl. Epoxy takes a while to set, but it's extremely strong.

6. Make sure to mark or eyeball the center of the bowl before gluing it to the canopy. An off-center bowl will fall over when you fill it with water. Set the birdbath aside long enough for the epoxy to cure.

7. Scout the perfect spot, place the birdbath, fill it up with water and enjoy your handiwork!

CRAFT: ALISON AUTH. PHOTO: HEIDI HESS

• • •

CITRONELLA CANDLES

Banish mosquitoes in style by making your own candles out of soy wax chips. Every little bit helps when it comes to repelling mosquitoes. Citronella candles are among the easiest, most pleasant ways to keep these insects at bay.

MATERIALS

- A few clean, dry glass jars
- Braided candlewick
- Hot glue
- Wooden dowel pieces
- Clothespins
- Natural soy wax chips
- Double boiler
- Old crayons or wax dye
- Citronella essential oil, found at natural food stores (not citronella-scented oil)

DIRECTIONS

1. For each jar, cut a braided wick a few inches longer than the jar's height. Dab a bit of hot glue to 1 end of the wick, and adhere glued end to the bottom center of your jar. When glue is set, wrap excess wick around a length of dowel you can lay across the top of the jar. (This will hold the wick straight.) Secure top of wick with a clothespin.

2. Pour wax chips into your double boiler, following the package instructions to melt the wax. As an alternative, you can make quicker work of this project by using microwaveable soy wax chips instead. These are fairly inexpensive and are available at many craft stores and a few discount department stores. If you go this route, be sure to use a microwave-safe bowl.

3. To color your candles, peel the paper off the crayons and chop them up. (The more crayons you use, the deeper the candles' color will be.) You can also use a wax dye to get your desired color. Either way, drop the dye pieces into melted wax and stir to incorporate.

4. Depending on the candle's size, add 5-10 drops of citronella essential oil for each candle you're making. Once the oil is stirred in, carefully pour the wax into your jars, being careful not to disturb the wicks.

5. Allow wax to cool completely before trimming excess wicks.

NOTE: Only use citronella candles outdoors. Never leave a lit candle unattended.

> **HANDMADE HELPER**
> Citronella works by masking the aromas that attract insects: carbon dioxide given off by our breathing, and the lactic acid produced naturally in our bodies.

TIN CAN LIGHTS

Entertaining in the evening? Turn various cans into fancy, funky, festive party lights.

MATERIALS

- Clean metal cans
- Paper, pencil and compass
- Ruler
- Measuring and adhesive tapes
- Thick wooden dowel
- Vise, pliers, hammer, large nail and drill
- 20- and 22-gauge tie wire (try copper or brass for extra sparkle)
- Work gloves
- Paint and paintbrush
- Candles

DIRECTIONS

1. Make a pattern of holes on paper to wrap around your can by using a photocopier to enlarge 1 of the 3 designs shown below. You can also cut a piece of paper to size and copy a design onto it freehand. Or, get creative and make your own original pattern!

2. To create your own circle design, use a compass and pencil to draw concentric circles and mark equidistant points around the outer edge. Draw lines from the center to these points to divide the circle into even sectors. A dot at each intersection indicates where a hole is to be made.

3. For a diamond design, draw a small diamond shape made of 2 equilateral triangles. Then, enclose this diamond in 2 proportionally larger triangles. Add dots to the outlines at evenly spaced intervals to indicate holes.

4. Tape the paper pattern to the can. Place 1 end of the dowel lengthwise in the vise; slip can over the other end.

5. At each dot on the pattern, make a divot in the can with a large nail (to help guide the drill), and then enlarge with a ⅛-in. drill bit. Make holes for the handles near the top of the can in the same way.

6. Make a handle by bending a 20-in. length of wire at its midpoint, then bending small hooks at each end to attach to can. Twist other end into a small loop for hanging. Paint cans if desired (avoid water-based or latex paints). Add candles and enjoy.

GLASS-JAR LIGHTS

Outdoor lighting doesn't have to be expensive or complicated to install. All you need are some everyday materials and a little imagination to set your summer get-together aglow.

MATERIALS

- Selection of glass jars
- 20- and 22-gauge tie wire (try copper or brass for extra sparkle)
- Vise, pliers and thick screwdriver
- Work gloves
- Measuring tape
- Glass paints and paintbrush
- Candles and sand

DIRECTIONS

1. Measure circumference of jar neck, add 3 in., and cut a piece of tie wire to this length. Bend the wire around the jar neck to form a loose circle, and use pliers to hook the 2 ends securely together. With a screwdriver, twist the wire to form 2 eye loops on opposite sides of the jar.

2. For the hanger, cut another piece of wire, 3 ft. long. At its midpoint, use pliers to twist a loop for hanging.

3. Thread 1 in. of each end of the hanger wire through the eye loops; secure the wire by twisting the ends back on themselves. If desired, embellish jar with glass paints, following the manufacturer's instructions. Make a bed of sand 2 in. deep in each jar, and insert a candle.

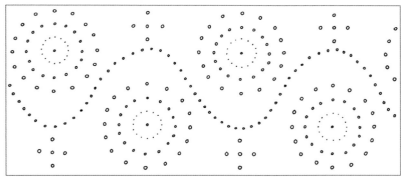

CIRCLE DESIGN

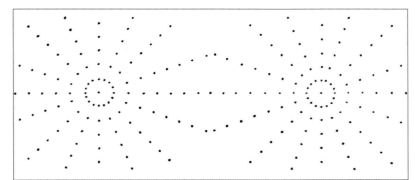

SUNBURST DESIGN

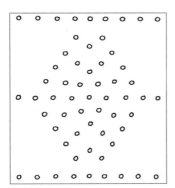

DIAMOND DESIGN

PVC PIPE FEEDER

Create this whimsical hummingbird feeder with materials you can find at your local hardware and craft stores. Decorate it in your favorite colors and the piece will serve double duty as a bird feeder and work of art.

MATERIALS

- **Three 9-in. lengths of ¾-in. PVC piping, each with threading at one end only**
- **6 PVC caps (3 slip, 3 threaded)**
- **Plumber's seal tape (if necessary)**
- **PVC adhesive**
- **Fine steel wool**
- **Drill and small bit**
- **Spray paint**
- **½-in. masking or painter's tape**
- **14-gauge copper wire**
- **Glass beads**
- **Fabric or plastic for flowers, or ready-made flowers (optional)**

DIRECTIONS

1. Using steel wool, lightly sand the pipe pieces and caps, including the insides of the slip caps.

2. Attach slip caps to the non-threaded end of the pipes with PVC adhesive. Allow to dry.

3. Drill a small hole in each piece of piping about 3 in. from the capped end.

4. Paint the PVC pipe. Prime it first or use a spray paint with primer. Spray on a base color and allow to dry. Create stripes by taping off a candy-cane pattern or other design and spraying with a second color. Create a zigzag stripe (as shown) by applying tape in the opposite direction of the first stripe and spraying with a third color. Allow each paint layer to dry completely before removing the tape.

5. Once paint is dry, wash pipes with mild soap and warm water to remove any paint odor or residue.

6. Cut a 22-in. length of wire and fold it in half, leaving an eye hook at the top. Twist the wire 5 times, add a glass bead and twist 5 more times. Wrap the 2 strands of wire around center of 1 pipe, twist 5 times, add a glass bead and twist 5 more times. Repeat for remaining pipes.

7. To hang the pipe pieces together, trim 1 wire at the end of the last twist, leaving a 1-in. tail on the other wire. Bend tail into a "C" to link the feeders (as shown on the pink feeder); flatten the "C" slightly with a hammer so the copper will hold its shape. To hang pieces individually, make a decorative swirl with wire ends (see blue and green feeders); flatten the swirls with a hammer.

8. Line everything up and tighten the wire around the tube. Tighten the twists until the tube is level and the hole faces up.

9. If desired, make a flower out of fabric or plastic. Put a hole in the center and glue to the outside of the feeding port.

10. Test feeder with water: Fill at the threaded end and close with a threaded cap. If it leaks, wrap the pipe threads with seal tape.

11. Fill feeder with nectar or sugar water, placing your finger over the feeding hole to prevent spilling. Seal with the threaded cap and hang feeder with the feeding holes facing up.

STEP 1

STEP 2

STEP 3

PRETTY POT TRELLIS

Hide an unsightly wall or dress up a drab fence with this lush, living wall of planted containers that can be made in a day.

You can change the look as often as you like—just unhook the pots and pop in fresh plants.

But before you head to the store or hit the workshop to build your trellis, measure the area you wish to cover. Then buy a trellis to suit the site or cut one to fit. You may wish to stain or paint it with exterior paint first. Then place the trellis in its spot, making sure the horizontal bars are sturdy enough to hold the weight of potted plants.

Follow the directions, and you'll have a great place to grow an herb garden or colorful wall of annuals.

MATERIALS

○ **Wood trellis, cut as needed**
○ **Clay pots, various sizes**
○ **Galvanized wire**
○ **Pliers**
○ **Potting soil**
○ **Plants or herbs of your choosing**

DIRECTIONS

1. To fashion a pot loop, bend a length of galvanized wire to fit snugly beneath each pot rim.
2. Twist 1 end of the wire over itself and pinch tight with pliers, leaving one long end free for hanging.
3. Bend the long end of the wire to make a hook that fits snugly over a horizontal piece of trellis.

• • •

DIVINE WAGON DIVAN

Transform the classic little red wagon into a welcoming outdoor seat that's moves wherever you need it. Whether you're doing fall yard cleanup or spring planting, this wagon lounge goes where you do.

MATERIALS

- Radio Flyer Classic Red Wagon with rim (any model)
- 4x8-ft. sheet of ⅝-in.-thick exterior-grade plywood
- 1x2-in. piece of wood for wagon perimeter
- 2x6-in. board cut to desired width of the bench seat and back
- 3-in. square posts
- Construction adhesive
- Wood screws
- Exterior latex semi-gloss primer and paint
- Jigsaw
- Screw gun

DIRECTIONS

Create the bench seat by flipping the wagon upside down and tracing its outline in pencil onto the plywood. Add 2⅝ in. to all sides; cut out with a jigsaw.

4. Cut another piece from the plywood that is slightly smaller than the interior dimensions of the wagon for a stabilizer panel. Screw the stabilizer panel to the center of the bench seat. Position bench seat on the wagon with the stabilizer panel inside.

5. Cut a 1x2-in. board long enough to surround the wagon's perimeter. Depending on the size of your wagon, you may need to use more than 1 board.

6. Screw the board to the underside of the bench where it hangs over the wagon rim. There should be a ⅝-in. space around the perimeter of the plywood. By sandwiching the wagon rim between the bench seat and board, the entire bench assemblage will be secured to the wagon. (Tip: This is easiest to do with the wagon assemblage upside down.)

7. Draw bench back onto the plywood and cut out with a jigsaw. The bench back should be the same width as the seat.

8. Cut a 2x6-in. board the width of the bench seat. Apply construction adhesive to the bottom of the board and attach to the back of the bench seat. Screw in place from the bottom of the bench seat and

the bench back to secure.

9. Cut armrests out of 3-in. posts. Apply construction adhesive and screw in place from the bottom of the bench seat, making sure the armrests are flush with the front of the bench seat and fit snugly against the bench back.

10. Measure and draw the decorative apron for the bench seat out of remaining plywood. Screw the decorative apron to the 1x2-in. board from Step 3. The apron should be flush with the front edge of the bench seat.

11. Prime and paint, then add your favorite cushions and pillows!

CRAFT: ALISON AUTH; PHOTO: HEIDI HESS

Bring in the
OUTDOORS

MAGIC KINGDOM

The details in this indoor fairy garden are adorable. Feel free to embellish your magic kingdom as you'd like!

MATERIALS

- Small birdhouse
- Adhesive sheets of moss
- Pastel scrapbook paper
- Thread spool
- Craft knife
- Needle-nose pliers
- Small saw
- Hot glue
- String
- Twigs and sticks in various sizes
- 6 to 8 large pine cones
- Acorn
- Wood slices in various heights and widths
- Optional: Loose moss, miniature silk flowers, pebbles, ground coffee, miniature bunnies and baskets, jelly beans, other dollhouse miniatures

DIRECTIONS

1. Design your fairy kingdom on paper. Decide how many wood slices you will need and in what sizes. Think about what embellishments you'd like to include.

2. Remove perch from birdhouse with a small saw. Using hot glue, create front door by embellishing the hole in the birdhouse with twigs and sticks. Create shutters in a similar fashion. Cover the exterior with moss sheets. Create flower boxes with loose moss and silk flowers if desired.

3. Starting at the bottom of a pine cone, use needle-nose pliers to remove scales. Build the roof by adhering the bottom row of pine cone scales around roofline of the house with hot glue. Shingle the next layer of scales, making sure that it overlaps the scales below it. Keep adding scales, 1 row at a time, removing any stray hot glue strings. Top off roof with an acorn cap.

4. Create trees by inserting a sturdy stick into hole of a thread spool. Secure with hot glue. Use hot glue to secure each tree to a wood slice; cover spool with sheet of moss. Hot-glue silk flowers to branches. Repeat with other sticks, thread spools and flowers as desired.

5. Arrange wood slices according to plan; cover tops of slices with moss sheets. Embellish with birdhouse and trees. If desired, use hot glue and pebbles to create pathways; add ground coffee to wood slices for soil. Add additional silk flowers and loose moss, bunnies, baskets, jelly beans, and/or dollhouse miniatures as desired.

6. For pennant banner, use craft knife to cut small triangles from scrapbook paper. Attach the triangles to string with hot glue. Tie between 2 tall points in your fairy garden.

CUTE CACTUS POTS

The perfect way to brighten up any spot, these adorable clay pots couldn't be easier. Choose paint colors that best reflect your decor.

MATERIALS

- **3 clay pots with saucers**
- **Sandpaper**
- **Sponge or soft rag**
- **Sponge brush**
- **Acrylic craft paints—white, metallic gold, green and red**
- **Paintbrushes**
- **Soft tape measure, optional**
- **Painter's tape**
- **3 plastic pot liners or clear acrylic spray varnish**
- **3 plants of choice**

DIRECTIONS

1. Clean and soak pots and saucers in warm water for 1 hour. Sand any rough edges and wipe clean with sponge or rag. Let dry completely.
2. Use a sponge brush to apply 2-3 coats of white acrylic paint to saucers and exterior of pots, letting paint dry after each application.
3. Use a paintbrush to adorn the top edge or rim of desired pots and saucers with metallic gold paint.
4. If desired, use soft tape measure to measure the circumference of pots. Use this measurement as a guide for determining the size and number of painted designs that fit around each pot.

HERRINGBONE DESIGN

Use pencil to mark angled lines in a continuous pattern around the center of pot. Use desired paintbrush to paint metallic gold and green lines as marked.

TRIANGLE DESIGN

Use pencil to mark a continuous triangle pattern around the bottom of a pot. Attach painter's tape along the sides of one triangle and paint with metallic gold. Dry completely: remove tape. Repeat until pattern is complete.

RANDOM DIAMOND DESIGN

Use a fine paintbrush to paint red diamond shapes freehand at random places around a pot. When dry, use fine paintbrush to paint a metallic gold border around each diamond.

Let pots dry completely. Line pots with plastic liners or follow varnish manufacturer's directions to apply 2 -3 coats of varnish to inside of pots, letting varnish dry after each application. Plant desired plant in each pot.

• • •

NATURE ON NATURE

Highlight autumn's hues on white or pale green pumpkins. Use one for a centerpiece or group several together.

MATERIALS

○ **Pumpkins**
○ **Fresh or thin silk leaves (see Note)**
○ **Decoupage glue**
○ **Sponge applicators**
○ **Small straight pins (optional)**

DIRECTIONS

1. If using silk leaves, tug away the fabric to detach the plastic spines and discard spines. Brush decoupage glue on an area of pumpkin slightly larger than a leaf. Carefully apply glue to back of leaf (Photo 1). Glue the leaf to the pumpkin, gently smoothing out as needed (Photo 2). If necessary, keep leaf flat with straight pins inserted slightly into the pumpkin.

2. Coat top of leaf with decoupage glue. Continue gluing leaves to the pumpkin until the design is complete. When dry, remove any pins and apply another 1-2 coats of decoupage glue to the entire pumpkin surface (Photo 3).

Note: If silk leaves are stiff or wrinkled, carefully iron with steam before applying.

PHOTO 1

PHOTO 2

PHOTO 3

SARAH LORRAINE EDWARDS. ADAPTED FROM NATURE ART WORKSHOP; PUBLISHED BY WALTER FOSTER PUBLISHING, AN IMPRINT OF THE QUARTO GROUP. QUARTOKNOWS.COM

MOSS LETTER ART

This easy project livens up any room.
Best of all, it never needs watering!

MATERIALS

- 8-in. papier-mache letter
- 8x10-in. frame
- 14x12-in. piece of burlap
- 18x16-in. piece of SuperMoss Instant Green Moss Mat
- Marker
- Glue gun
- Brads

DIRECTIONS

1. Set letter on the back of the moss mat and trace the shape with a marker. Cut out and hot-glue to the front of the letter.
2. Measure the thickness of the letter and cut strips of equal width from moss mat. Hot-glue the strips to the sides of the letter.
3. Remove glass from frame.
4. Cover the backing board with burlap and trim to size. Glue to board at corners.
5. Apply hot glue to the back of the letter and place the letter in the center of the burlap-covered board.
6. When dry, flip the board over and hammer brads into the back of the letter about 4 in. apart.
7. Place the backing in the frame and secure in place.

HANDMADE HELPER
Burlap adds a warm feel to the background, but use a solid swatch of material or a design if you'd like.

MINI CORK PLANTERS

Make a tiny garden that easily attaches to your fridge, file cabinet or other metal surface with magnets. Use plants that don't need much water or soil, such as succulents.

MATERIALS

- 6-10 natural wine corks
- Small succulents or air plants
- Cactus or succulent soil mix
- Screwdriver or awl
- Craft knife
- Tacky glue
- Small magnets (about ½ in.)

DIRECTIONS

1. Using the screwdriver or awl, punch a hole about two-thirds of the way down in 1 end of each cork. Use the knife to enlarge the hole to about ¼ in. wide.
2. Glue 2-3 magnets to the side of each cork; let dry.
3. Fill the hole in each cork with a pinch of soil. Then add the plant and, if needed, more soil.
4. Place on fridge or other metal surface. Water lightly as needed, or spritz with a water bottle.

MEMORY JAR

Preserve the fun of a family vacation by collecting mementos in a Mason jar.

MATERIALS

○ **Mason jar with lid**
○ **Twine or ribbon**
○ **Soil mix or sand**
○ **Optional: Photographs, dollhouse miniatures, scrapbook paper**

DIRECTIONS

1. Fill bottom of Mason jar with soil or sand collected from vacation spot. Add a photo from the trip, as well as some trinkets or natural items you found along the way. Embellish display with dollhouse miniatures, if desired.

2. Use scrapbook paper to create a label in or on the jar to note the location and date of the trip. Top with lid and tie some twine or ribbon around the top to finish the look.

COUNTRY PLACE MATS

Bring a bit of country to your table with these cute and casual upcycled mats.

MATERIALS

○ ½ yd. denim fabric
○ Heavy-duty thread
○ Back pocket from old jeans
○ Sewing machine
○ Iron

DIRECTIONS

1. Cut denim to preferred place mat size, about 12x18 in. Using heavy-duty thread, sew a ½-in. border around denim.

2. Iron mat and trim any loose strings.

3. Sew the pocket on 3 sides to lower right side of mat, keeping top open. Sew along existing stitching on pocket. Tuck silverware and a napkin in pocket.

• • •

TIN CAN HERB SET

Relish spring and summer every day with a delightful tabletop herb garden.

MATERIALS

- 3 recycled soup cans
- Metal pie plate
- 3 herb plants
- Potting soil
- Small decorative rocks
- Burlap ribbon, extra wide
- Burlap lace ribbons, various widths
- Jute twine
- 3 flat wood ovals
- 3 wood skewers
- Card stock scraps
- 3 oval stickers, black
- Fine-point paint pen, white
- Drill
- Glue gun
- Craft glue

1. Remove labels from the cans. Wash cans with soap and water, removing any label residue.

2. Drill a small hole through the bottom of each can for drainage. Repot each plant in a can, adding potting soil as needed.

3. Wrap a piece of extra wide ribbon around each can; overlap ends. Fold overlapping edge under to create a hem; hot-glue hem.

4. Wrap a piece of lace ribbon around the wide ribbon on each can, varying the lace widths among the cans, and glue as in Step 3, positioning the overlapped ends over the previous ends.

5. Trace wood oval on wide burlap ribbon and cut out 3 burlap ovals. Using craft glue, adhere a burlap oval to each wood oval, matching edges. Trim edges to neaten, if needed.

6. Hot-glue a border of twine around the burlap oval edges for a finished look.

7. For each plant marker, use paint pen to write an herb name on a sticker. Attach the sticker to a card stock scrap, and trim card edge even with the sticker. Hot-glue the sticker assembly to the center of a burlap oval.

8. Hot-glue the blunt end of a skewer to the back of each assembled herb marker. Let dry completely.

9. Place plants in pie plate. Add markers. Arrange rocks around cans in a pie plate as desired.

> **HANDMADE HELPER**
> If burlap and lace aren't your style, use any fabric and ribbon combo you like. Or spray-paint the outside of the cans for a sleek look.

INDEX